Getting Inside
the Bible

Getting Inside
the Bible

by Herbert H. Lambert

The Bethany Press

St. Louis   Missouri

The scripture quotations in this publication are from the Revised Standard
Version of the Bible, copyrighted 1946, 1952, © 1971, 1973 by the
Division of Christian Education of the National Council of the Churches
of Christ in the U.S.A., and used by permission.

Cover art by Dorothy Sappington

for Esther

Library of Congress Cataloging in Publication Data
Lambert, Herbert H   1929-
   Getting inside the Bible.

   1. Bible—Introductions. I. Title.
BS475.2.L27   220.6   76-10325
ISBN 0-8272-1218-6

Manufactured in the U.S.A.

Preface

This book is written for persons who want to understand and enjoy the Bible but have found some difficulty in doing so. They may have begun reading the Bible several times but have become discouraged because it seems so long and so obscure. Even those books of the Bible, such as the Gospels, which are easy to read may contain parts that are difficult for most readers to interpret. And almost every reader of the Bible must ask again and again what this collection of writings, completed so many centuries ago, has to do with our life today.

Because I think such concerns deserve specific answers, I have selected a few representative sections of the Bible for interpretation in this book. I begin with two of the leters of Paul in order to show the interesting persons and circumstances that lie behind the bare text. Chapters 2 through 6 deal with old Testament portions. Chapters 7 and 8 return to the New Testament. I saved Deuteronomy for Chapter 9 because it deals with the lasting importance of tradition. I felt that by the time the reader completes the first eight chapters, he or she will understand why I agree with Deuteronomy. Also, in the earlier chapters I wanted to show the Bible as a fascinating book to read. In Chapter 9, I wanted to show the Bible as something more—a source of something absolutely necessary for existence itself.

The final chapter is intended as a springboard for responsible and meaningful Bible study. This book is too short to pretend to be a complete introduction to the Bible. But it could be an introduction to Bible study, showing persons how to obtain and use some of the excellent books about the Bible which are available and providing a helpful way of approaching the Bible itself. One feature of this final chapter is the suggestion that the reader needs to decide what kind of Bible student he or she wishes to be. It offers guidance for maximizing one's experience within the four areas of competency which are explained in this chapter.

I have called the book *Getting Inside the Bible* because I think we need to do more than simply read the words of the Bible and become familiar with them. I think we need to become acquainted with the persons who wrote the Bible and the deeply human experiences out of which they wrote. In this way the Bible will become a living book for us, one that also speaks to the concerns, frustrations, and hopes of our time.

In order to help the reader get the sequence of events and persons in order, I have devised a simple time line which is used several times in this book.

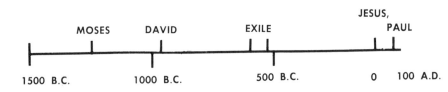

Contents

Chapter 1

A Book
About Real People

The Bible was written by and about persons much like ourselves, subject to the same misfortunes and opportunities and impelled by similar hopes. The book becomes dull for us only if we approach it as a dull book. One mistake we make is to start at Genesis with the intention of reading straight through to Revelation. Reading thus becomes a chore or a pious duty. Little wonder that all but the most dedicated give up before reaching Deuteronomy, and those who persist frequently do not understand what they are reading.

The Bible was not written from Genesis to Revelation, and there is no reason why it must be read that way. It is like a library of different kinds of material from which the user takes what is interesting or useful at the moment. I would suggest that you begin with a portion of scripture that interests you and then proceed to other parts when they appeal to you. You may secure one of the little bound volumes marked "Journal" in a variety store and use it to keep permanent notes on your reading. Write down a few impressions as you read. Reserve the first page or two to list the books of the Bible you have studied. Some time in the future you may decide to consult this list and then read any remaining books that you have not yet studied.

A Slave Who Became a Bishop

One way to begin studying the Bible is to read the shortest of the sixty-six books, Philemon. In most Bibles it occupies less than a single page. What are your impressions on reading Philemon? You may recognize the names of Paul and Timothy, but the others are probably unfamiliar to you. Paul seems to be praising Philemon and also making a request, but it is not clear what Paul wants Philemon to do. There is much more to this letter than the casual reader can discover without help.

The Letter to Philemon is part of a story about three men whose lives were intertwined and who were profoundly affected by the Spirit of Christ, each in a different way. Scholars who have attempted to reconstruct the story are not in complete agreement about the details. I will give my interpretation, and those who wish to pursue the matter further may consult the notes on this chapter at the back of the book.[1]

In the Lycus Valley of western Asia Minor lay the town of Colossae. A little more than twenty years after the crucifixion of Jesus, there appeared here a preacher named Paul of Tarsus. Speaking in the marketplace, he convinced a number of persons that Jesus of Nazareth had come from God to offer them salvation. These persons formed a small congregation which Paul organized and then left after a few days or weeks. The group included slaves and masters, poor persons and wealthy ones. One of the latter was a man named Philemon, who offered his own house as a meeting place for the new congregation. Philemon also helped the group of Christians by his hopeful and expectant attitude. We know about a minister at Colossae named Archippus, who may well have been the son of Philemon.

It often happened that when a wealthy person like Philemon became a Christian, his whole household, including slaves and children, were baptized. But at least one person in Philemon's house did not become a Christian. He was the young slave named Onesimus, which means useful. Why did Onesimus refuse to be baptized? Perhaps he wanted to see what difference the new religion would make in the people who adhered to it. When the white missionaries attempted to convert the Seneca Indians of New York State, Chief Red Jacket urged the missionaries to go to the white settlers instead. If the latter became more kind and

10

loving toward Indians, Red Jacket said, he and his followers would consider becoming Christian. In somewhat the same spirit, Onesimus may have waited to see how his master and the other Christians acted before deciding whether or not he himself wanted to be a Christian.[2]

Years passed, and still Onesimus did not become a Christian. He watched the little group which met for prayers in Philemon's house, but he remained unmoved. Enmity between him and his master grew. Philemon became so disgusted with the slave that he nicknamed the young man "Useless" instead of "Useful." And while Philemon was greatly respected among the Christians of Colossae and elsewhere, Onesimus knew a side of his nature which was hidden to the public. We have a proverb that no man is a hero to his valet, and Philemon seemed like a hypocrite to his slave Onesimus.

Onesimus finally decided to run away. He took some of his master's money, went down to the seacoast, and took passage on a ship bound for Rome.[3] He went in this direction for two reasons. The teeming city of Rome would be a good place in which to escape detection. People of all nations would be massed there, and no one would ask questions about his place of origin. Also, he had heard the news that Paul of Tarsus was now in Rome. Onesimus needed more than freedom and money. He needed someone he could trust, someone with whom he could have a meaningful personal relationship. The one person he could trust was Paul of Tarsus. He had seen the man only briefly, perhaps once or twice years before, but like many others Onesimus could not forget Paul. After that first meeting Onesimus remembered Paul as a possible friend in time of need.

When Onesimus found Paul, the apostle was under guard awaiting his trial before the Emperor. At the same time, he was allowed to send and receive letters, to receive and disburse funds, to talk with visitors, and to supervise from a distance the affairs of some of the churches he had founded. Paul needed some trustworthy helpers, and Onesimus quickly became one of these. At last Onesimus also became a Christian. A deep relationship developed between him and Paul, so that Paul said the young man seemed to him like his very own heart.

Did Onesimus tell Paul about running away and taking the money? If so, it seems somewhat strange that some time passed before Paul attempted to send Onesimus back to his master. Perhaps the apostle wisely waited until passions had cooled before attempting a reconciliation. It has also been suggested that Onesimus did not tell Paul the whole story. He may even have posed as an emissary of Philemon, coming with his permission and blessing. If Onesimus did attempt such a deception, it must have fallen apart with the arrival in Rome of Epaphras, the minister from Colossae. Epaphras would have told Paul the facts in the case.[1]

Paul felt it necessary to remove the enmity between his two friends, Onesimus and Philemon. He knew also that a shadow and even a punishment awaited Onesimus when his crime became known. He wanted to restore the man's peace and if possible obtain his freedom. It may seem strange to us that Paul did not condemn slavery as such or encourage slaves to run away. If he had done this, he would have brought down upon his head official condemnation without achieving any lasting result. What Paul thought about the institution of slavery is not clear, but he did try to improve the relationship between slaves and their masters. He may have been thinking about Onesimus when he wrote to the church at Colossae:

> Slaves, obey in everything those who are your earthly masters, not with eyeservice, as men-pleasers, but in singleness of heart, fearing the Lord. Whatever your task, work heartily, as serving the Lord and not men, knowing that from the Lord you will receive the inheritance as your reward; you are serving the Lord Christ. For the wrongdoer will be paid back for the wrong he has done, and there is no partiality. Masters, treat your slaves justly and fairly, knowing that you also have a Master in heaven. (Col. 3:22—4:1)

While Paul made no direct attack on slavery, the respect for persons which he and others preached helped to bring about its eventual end.

Paul decided to send Onesimus back to Colossae in the company of Tychicus. There was considerable risk in doing this because Paul knew that Philemon was angry. By law he had the right to do anything he chose with the runaway slave. Onesimus could be branded with the letter "F" for the Latin term meaning fugitive, so that others would see his shame perpetually. He could even be severely punished or killed. Paul decided to send Onesimus accompanied by a letter which, he hoped, would save him from Philemon's wrath. He prayed that the latter would hold his temper long enough to read the letter!

You may now read the letter to Philemon again. Notice how much meaning it now has for you in the light of what we have just learned. It is a masterpiece of diplomacy. In twenty-five short verses, Paul brings all of his powers of persuasion to bear upon Philemon. He applies just enough pressure to achieve the desired result without antagonizing his friend. He attempts to picture the situation as an opportunity rather than as an impertinent demand. He shows that he considers the matter serious, but he tries to avoid lecturing Philemon about his Christian duty.

Paul speaks of the "love" and "faith" of Philemon of which he has heard. No doubt he has heard of other qualities from the lips of Onesimus, but he tactfully forgets about these. Here Paul uses the utmost skill in bringing out the best side of Philemon's character. We do not really know what Philemon was like, but if he was as kind as Paul suggests in this letter there would have been no need for the letter. Indeed, Onesimus would probably not have run away in the first place.

Robert Browning had a way of looking on the best side of the worst people. Chesterton called him "a kind of cosmic detective who walked into the foulest of thieves' kitchens and accused men publicly of virtue."[5] But Browning was sometimes naive about the people he described. Paul, on the other hand, knew both the evil and the good of which persons are capable. He tried to bring out the better side of Philemon by challenging him to be consistently what he was able to be occasionally. The ancient philosopher Diogenes carried a lantern in daylight, looking vainly, he said, for an honest man. Paul found some honest and loving persons by taking a second look into the hearts of ordinary persons like ourselves. Paul knew that a person is not just what he or she appears to be at the moment but also what he or she can become.

Paul hoped that Philemon would receive his slave and welcome him as a brother in Christ, not just because Paul demanded it but of his own free choice (with a little help from Paul's persuasive letter). Paul offered to pay back what Onesimus had taken, but at the same time he indicated that he did not think Philemon would have the gall to ask for payment from one to whom he himself owed much. There is even the suggestion that Philemon might send Onesimus back to Rome so that he could continue to work with Paul. Paul also indicates that he hopes to visit Colossae soon. This mention of an impending visit may have been intended as a warning to Philemon that Paul would be coming personally to see whether or not his suggestions were being followed.

What happened as a result of this masterful letter, so full of urgency and tact, of Christian love and human insight? There is no definitive answer, but there are tantalizing clues. The fact that the letter was preserved by those who received it must mean that its contents were not rejected. About fifty years after the letter was written, Ignatius, Bishop of Antioch, was arrested and taken to Rome for execution. As he stopped in various towns in Asia Minor, church officials traveled to speak with him and say farewell. One of these was an old bishop from Ephesus named Onesimus! Was it the slave who had been converted by Paul? This is possible, especially when we consider some additional facts.[6]

A few years before Ignatius passed through Asia Minor, the letters of Paul were collected and published. This act, so fateful for the history of Christianity, so important for the development of the New Testament, was probably done at Ephesus, where Onesimus was bishop. Included in the collection was one short letter which, unlike the others, was addressed to an individual. It contains no great doctrine, and there is little reason for its inclusion unless someone had a personal reason for wanting it to be included. If the chief person responsible for the collecting and publishing of Paul's letters was the same Onesimus mentioned in the Letter to Philemon, we have the reason for its inclusion in the collection.

What was Bishop Onesimus like in his later years? Here is what Ignatius writes to the Christians at Ephesus:

> I hope, indeed, by your prayers to have the good fortune to fight with the wild beasts in Rome, so that by doing so I can be a real disciple. In God's name, therefore, I received your large congregation in the person of Onesimus, your bishop in this world, a man whose love is beyond words. My prayer is that you shall love him in the spirit of Jesus Christ and all be like him. Blessed is He who let you have such a bishop. You deserved it.[7]

We have now met some of the real people on a single page of the Bible, and in my copy we have nine hundred and eighty other pages to examine. We will not be able to discuss all of them at such length, but we will consider many more pages and many more persons as we attempt to get inside the Bible and understand its message.

A Letter from Death Row

Can you imagine yourself in prison? Suppose you were involved, like Paul, in a riot because some people were under the mistaken impression that you had done something to offend them. Suppose the authorities arrested you instead of the people who were seeking to harm you. Imagine that you tried to explain the true situation to one judge after another, only to have them shake their heads in incomprehension. Suppose you appealed your case to the highest court and after years in prison were still not vindicated, with the strong chance that you might never get out of prison alive. Suppose that you were on death row. What kind of letter would you write to your friends? It might go something like this:

14

Dear Friends at Philippi:

Sometimes I get so discouraged that I think God has deserted me. Why does he treat me this way? As for those heartless people who put me here, I hope they get what they deserve! When I think of the possibility of my being put to death, it fills me with fear and anxiety. I appreciate your concern for me, but there is little you can do. What a fool I was to let myself get into this mess! Sometimes I get so upset about the future that I wish it were all over for me.

Something like this is what we might expect, but Paul's letter to the Philippians is quite different!

It seems likely that Paul wrote the Letter to the Philippians from Rome near the end of his life.⁸ If so, it may have been written shortly after he wrote to Philemon regarding his slave Onesimus. In Acts 16 we read that Paul, some ten years earlier, traveled to Philippi and gathered a small group of persons who wanted to be followers of Christ. One of them was a woman named Lydia, a seller of purple goods. Another was the jailer who guarded Paul at Philippi during one of his many imprisonments. As you read the letter, notice how much affection the apostle shows toward his friends in Philippi.

This letter shows four unusual characteristics, considering that it was written by a prisoner on death row. First, *the writer shows unusual concern for other persons.* Of the 104 verses in the letter, 86 demonstrate appreciation for or interest in someone besides the writer himself. How many of your own letters can score as high?

Philippians is a kind of love letter in which the writer heaps phrase on phrase to express his sincere affection for his readers. Paul yearns for his friends and thanks God for them in every prayer (1:3, 8). He does not know whether he will soon die or not, but he is not greatly concerned. There is one reason why he would like to live a little longer—so that he can see and help the Philippians (1:22-26).

In chapter 4, Paul speaks of the money which his friends sent to him by Epaphroditus. This is just the latest of several gifts they have sent to him. He says again and again that he does not need the money, but he appreciates the gesture and believes that the act of giving will benefit those who give (4:11, 17). Notice how eloquently Paul expresses gratitude to the Philippians in this chapter while denying that he himself has any pressing needs.

Paul calls some of his Philippian friends by name. How we

would like to know what the quarrel was between those two women, Euodia and Syntyche (4:2)! Who was the "true yoke-fellow" whom Paul asked to help them (4:3)? Paul was concerned about the illness of Epaphroditus, the messenger from Philippi, and afraid that his friends would worry about him during his long absence (2:25-30). Paul speaks highly of his helper Timothy and promises to send him to them soon (2:19-22).

Here, then, is a person who has put aside his own anxieties and has written a letter full of love and concern for his friends. We sense the warmth of these words, even though at this distance it is hard for us to know exactly what Paul meant. But why should we expect to understand a private letter between close friends? Do you feel a little guilty reading another person's mail like this? It may help you to know that some of those who received the letter were still alive when the letter was published and no doubt gave their consent. None of the letters Paul wrote were intended by him to become part of a book. He would have been surprised to know that millions would regard them as inspired scripture.

A second surprising fact about this letter written from death row is *the way in which the writer thinks of himself.* Take a few minutes now to read Philippians 3:2-17 and 4:11-13. "Confidence in the flesh" here means self-satisfaction which comes from having obeyed ritual laws, such as those requiring circumcision and the observance of the sabbath. Such confidence may also come from having been born into the "right" family, one chosen by God to receive his blessing.

From your reading of these verses, would you characterize Paul as groveling, smug, conceited, selfish, humble, dependent on Christ, grateful for God's help, self-satisfied, self-critical, self-confident, or despondent? Underline those words and phrases in the last sentence which seem to describe the attitude of Paul in this letter. It is not easy to decide because Paul seems to be both boastful and humble. He is certainly not paralyzed with self-pity, fear, or guilt. He is confident and strong. Yet he is conscious that he is not yet perfect, and he knows that he is wholly dependent on Christ. When he compared himself with certain Jewish Christians who boasted of their righteousness and obedience to the Old Testament law, Paul said, "I'm as good as they are, if not better" (3:4 paraphrased). But when he contemplated how little this really matters in God's sight, he felt no sense of pride or satisfaction (3:7-8).

Christians have reason to feel good about themselves, not because of what they are or have done but because of what Christ

16

offers them and of what he is able to do through them. It is not always easy for Christians to evaluate themselves without falling into despair, on the one hand, or becoming smug and self-satisfied, on the other. Yet Paul avoided both of these pitfalls. An eighteenth-century missionary to the American Indians, David Brainerd, kept a diary in which he berated himself for his many sins. Reading it today, we wonder why an Indian or anyone else would be attracted to the faith and way of life proclaimed by this Christian. How different is the attitude of Paul, who rejoices in his own achievements and yet attributes all of them to the presence of Christ in his life!

A third unexpected feature of this letter from death row is *the spirit of optimism which pervades it.* How many times would you guess that Paul uses the words "joy" and "rejoice" in these 104 verses? After you have made an estimate, you may want to count the number to see how close you came.⁹ How could someone in danger of death write such a happy letter? Paul indicates that he was expecting death to come at any time (1:21-23; 2:17). Concern for his friends may have kept him from telling them how likely this prospect may have been as he wrote. Yet Paul was not consumed with foreboding or self-pity. He thought of death as another great opportunity, the chance to be with Christ at last. His only regret about death was the fact that it would take him away from his friends and keep him from serving their needs. Did any other prisoner ever think such thoughts or write such words as these?

Paul saw his imprisonment not as a catastrophe but as a unique opportunity. He could tell the Roman guards about Christ, and his strength in spite of affliction would have a good influence on many persons. It would give courage to other Christians as they contemplated Paul's example (1:12-14). There were preachers of the gospel who envied Paul and saw his misfortune as a chance to get ahead of him. Even this did not perturb Paul, for he thought only of the fact that the gospel was being proclaimed (1:15-18). Almost no circumstance or event could mar the serenity or dim the hopefulness which characterized this prisoner.

I recall reading Philippians 4:8-9 when I was a freshman in college. I was in deep financial and personal difficulty. Turning to the Bible for guidance, I found these words of encouragement. But they seemed hollow and meaningless to me. Knowing little about the writer and the circumstances under which he wrote, I assumed that he knew little about real life. The words seemed as empty as those of Queen Marie Antoinette, who, when told that her subjects were without bread, replied, "Let them eat cake."

Paul's words in Philippians seemed like good advice from someone who knew little about difficulty. I considered them to be pious rubbish.

But the suggestion to "think about these things" did not come from a dreamer in an ivory tower. They were composed out of a full heart by a prisoner on death row. From an earlier letter we take this description of his experiences:

> Five times I have received at the hands of the Jews the forty lashes less one. Three times I have been beaten with rods; once I was stoned. Three times I have been shipwrecked; a night and a day I have been adrift at sea; on frequent journeys, in danger from rivers, danger from robbers, danger from my own people, danger from Gentiles, danger in the city, danger in the wilderness, danger at sea, danger from false brethren; in toil and hardship, through many a sleepless night, in hunger and thirst, often without food, in cold and exposure. And, apart from other things, there is the daily pressure upon me of my anxiety for all the churches. (2 Corinthians 11:24-28)

How can we fail to take seriously the heartening words of such a person? Consider again his words in the Philippian letter, in the light of the sufferings described above and the probability that he was writing from death row:

> Whatever is true, whatever is honorable, whatever is just, whatever is pure, whatever is lovely, whatever is gracious, if there is any excellence, if there is anything worthy of praise, think about these things. (4:8)

What did Jesus look like? What was the color of his eyes and the shape of his nose? It would cause a sensation if archeologists were to unearth somewhere in the sands of Palestine an authentic picture of him. But in the Letter of Paul to the Philippians we have a fascinating portrait of Jesus to examine now. It does not tell of his physical appearance but describes who he is and what he does. It tells of his significance for Christians. This is the fourth remarkable feature of this letter, its *description of Jesus as servant and Lord*.

Nathaniel Hawthorne told the story of Ernest, a young man who grew up in a valley beneath a mountain crag known as the Great Stone Face. He had been told that some day a person of great virtue would appear whose features would resemble the stone figure on the mountain. Ernest's hopes were raised when a famous resident returned, Mr. Gathergold, the wealthy merchant. Again, he looked for the likeness in the face of Old Blood-and-Thunder, the noted general. Finally, Ernest observed the face of Stony Phiz, the politician. But none of these had captured the strength and beauty of the Great Stone Face. Instead, it was

18

Ernest himself, the meditative young man who looked at and wondered about the face year after year, who at last came to bear its features. In the Philippian letter, Paul drew a picture of Jesus and called upon his readers to look thoughtfully upon it so that they might come to resemble its beautiful image. There are hints of jealousy and selfishness among the Philippians, and Paul wants to displace this with the unselfish service shown in the example of Christ.

"Fill up my cup of happiness by thinking and feeling alike," Paul writes, "with the same love for one another, the same turn of mind, and a common care for unity. There must be no room for rivalry and personal vanity among you, but you must humbly reckon others better than yourselves. Look to each other's interest and not merely to your own. Let your bearing towards one another arise out of your life in Christ Jesus." (2:2-5, *New English Bible*[10]) The description of Christ which follows this has been compared to a ladder. Jesus came down it and then went up it again:

Down the Ladder

For the divine nature was his from the first;
yet he did not think to snatch at equality with God,
but made himself nothing,
assuming the nature of a slave.
Bearing the human likeness,
revealed in human shape,
he humbled himself,
and in obedience accepted even death—death on a cross.

Up the Ladder

Therefore God raised him to the heights
and bestowed on him the name above all names,
that at the name of Jesus every knee should bow—
in heaven, on earth, and in the depths—
and every tongue confess, 'Jesus Christ is Lord,'
to the glory of God the Father. (2:6-11 NEB)

Was Jesus a human being, or was he divine Lord and Savior? The answer here is clearly both. There were some early Christians who found it difficult to believe that Jesus really became a man. They said that he only "seemed" to be a man. Ignatius countered with the statement that anyone who speaks this way only "seems" to be a Christian. Real Christians accept Jesus as a real man—not part man and part God, but completely and genuinely human at the same time that he is fully and really divine.

Paul writes in Philippians that Jesus by his own choice became

19

a human person like us. More than that, he humbled himself still further and became a slave, one who serves others in a lowly role. More than that, he became a victim of a cruel death. He submitted to the death of a criminal in order to show God's love to us.

Jesus came all the way down the ladder for us! In contrast, most of us spend all our lives trying to get up the ladder—trying to advance in our careers, to get more income, to outdo our neighbors. Thomas Hardy tells of two girls who grew up in an English coastal town. One married a businessman, and each year she seemed to have more to spend. The other girl married a sailor who provided her with a house but few luxuries. She was jealous of her companion who had married the merchant, and she urged her husband to go back to sea even after his retirement so that she would have more money to spend. Still her friend got ahead of her in worldly goods. Finally, the sailor's wife persuaded her two sons to join her husband at sea in order to swell the family income. The three men were lost in a storm at sea, and the jealous, striving woman was left to spend her years in poverty and loneliness.[11]

Jesus came all the way down the ladder, and because he did this willingly for us, God lifted him back up the ladder. Remember how Joseph was hated by his brothers. They tried to kill him and then sold him into slavery. But God protected Joseph in Egypt, and he became an important official. In the end, Joseph's brothers became dependent on him and looked to him for help. Similarly, Jesus suffered much from his enemies but was then lifted up to the very throne of God. Christians regard him no longer as a slave or a criminal but as Lord of their lives.

The word translated "Lord" in the New Testament was used in the ancient world to mean a dictator, one who was to be obeyed at pain of death under all circumstances. Lord of the world could only mean one who, like Alexander, had conquered all men and demanded their complete allegiance. In our century we have known men who have ruled large parts of the world in such a way. We do not think much of them because they were cruel and because their power prevented the free growth of those who lived under it. It is good that we are reluctant to honor any human being, however capable, as our ruler. But Jesus is different. He is absolutely wise and completely kind. He would not command anything that would harm or destroy us. He deserves our complete obedience as no earthly leader does. His rule in our lives does not stifle our growth but brings us to mature personhood. To serve him completely is to be completely free.

20

There are different kinds of leaders among us. Some of them seem to withdraw themselves from everyday life. We seldom see or hear from them. We may suspect that they do not want to associate with ordinary people. When Cardinal Wolsey walked among the common people of London, he held half an orange to his nose in order to counteract the odors. Others do not go as far as this but seem to have the same fear of contamination. Jesus, on the other hand, was a very approachable leader. His willingness to associate with the lowly made him something of a scandal among the scribes and Pharisees. Jesus was one of us before he became what he is for us today. We may visit him and be recognized, just as an old friend from back home may visit a governor or a congressman and be welcomed. We talk to Jesus about our everyday experiences, and he understands us because he has shared many of them himself. And because he is much more than simply one of us, he is able to offer us real help. The picture which Paul drew in prison shows Jesus as humble servant and exalted Lord. The two sides of this picture belong together.

But Paul found that his best plans had gone astray. He had dreamed great dreams and made long preparations for the future of his work. He had wanted to carry the gospel to the distant shores of Spain (Rom. 15:28). But this was not to be. How easily could Paul have been consumed with bitterness and disappointment during his last hours! If life thus ends in frustration, doesn't the rest of it become meaningless, a mere exercise on a treadmill? Paul did not think so. He saw even the disappointment and hardship of prison as a kind of prelude, an overture to the main performance, for which even its tragic theme was a superb preparation.

The Letter to the Philippians is a kind of Hallelujah Chorus of glory and honor and power and praise to the One who eternally is and ever shall be. It is not the shallow, mocking laughter that tries to mask the emptiness of things. It is quiet confidence that looks into the face of the hangman and says, "For me to live is Christ, and to die is gain." It is not a game of "Let's Pretend" that seeks to make a diverting game of the days that oppress us with their frightful possibilities. In an old newsreel from 1944, soldiers danced in an English beer hall the night before they sailed for Brittany, many never to return alive. There is something eerie and unreal about their gaiety. But the exuberance Paul expressed in Philippians is not just whistling in the dark. It is the calm expectancy of one who believes in the love and power of God. "If there be any virtue, if there be anything worthy of praise, think about these things."

Chapter 2

How It All Began

When I travel to my favorite camping spot at Silver Mines, a hundred miles south of St. Louis, I travel back a billion years in time. In the deep cuts along the highway may be seen layers of coal, limestone, and sandstone deposited here over millions of years. I can stop the car and find the fossil outlines of tiny shelled creatures who lived here when this area was under water. As I drive higher into the Ozark Plateau, I find earlier layers of sediment, now exposed by long periods of erosion. At Silver Mines, I stand at last on the ancient crust of the earth. Through its broken and buckled surface runs a dark streak made by molten rock which once surged up from the fiery depths.

Much can be learned about the age and origin of the earth by observing rocks. Much can be learned about the development of plant and animal life by gathering examples from all over the world and then comparing and classifying them. How can this knowledge be reconciled with what we find in the early chapters of Genesis? Genesis speaks of the world and its inhabitants being created in six days. It is true that "day" is sometimes used in the Old Testament to mean an indefinite period of time, but Genesis 1:5 seems to make clear that an ordinary day of twenty-four hours is intended here. In Genesis, light is created before the sun, moon, and stars, as though it did not come to us from them. Everything comes into existence at the command of God, not through a long process of development according to a natural pattern of cause and effect.

According to Genesis, creation took place at one time in the past, while we think of it as still going on. Terms such as firmament, heavens, waters, and "the deep" point to a view of the world quite different from the one with which we are familiar. Man, according to Genesis, was created by a special act of God. Science envisions a gradual development of animal life from simple forms, to vertebrates and man-like species, and finally, hundreds of thousands of years ago, to man as we know him.

Many Christians assume that, if there is a contradiction between the statements in Genesis and the conclusions we draw from examining rocks and living forms, then our conclusions must be at fault. Perhaps God placed the fossils in the rocks on purpose to deceive us! In any case, Genesis cannot be in error. If it can be mistaken in a single detail, then the whole Bible may be called in question. The basic teachings of the Christian faith —that God is our Father and that we are to love our neighbors —seem to be on shaky ground if we have doubts about other parts of the Book which proclaims these teachings. If parts of the Bible are inaccurate, these Christians say, then the reader is forced to decide what parts to accept. Then he or she is no longer relying on the Bible for guidance but on reason or personal whim. No, these Christians say, we must accept the whole Bible as inspired and therefore infallible.

The reasoning in the above paragraph is persuasive, but it may be based on some mistaken premises. We would like to have a Bible which is free from error, but are we sure that God requires such a Bible? We would like God to speak to us in simple language so that there need be no discussion of what is meant, but do we know that God always speaks to us in this way? We may agree that God could, if he chose, overcome the human limitations of those who wrote the Bible, but do we know that God actually chose to do so?

In the last chapter we found that Paul, guided by a remarkable faith, was able to write letters which we acknowledge as scripture. Nevertheless, he was still subject to human limits. He did not know whether or not Philemon would forgive Onesimus. He did not know whether he was to be executed or whether he would be released from prison. If Paul, a writer of many books in the New Testament, was thus limited, why may not the writers of Genesis also have been limited? Why not assume that they lacked information about the age of the earth and the process by which plants, animals, and man came into existence? It may well be that God chose to send an important message through these writers at the same time that he left them ignorant of many truths known to us today.

Let us go to the Bible to discover what it is, not to confirm what we have already assumed that it must be. Let us see what God has done and said in this book. Let us gather all the facts which are found in the book itself and other information which bears upon the Bible from history and archeology. Then let us decide which explanations best fit all the known facts. This is the method by which a geologist decides the age and origin of the rocks between St. Louis and Silver Mines. The same method can be applied to Bible study. In fact, this way of examining the Bible has been used intensively for more than two centuries. Those who have used the method are in remarkable agreement about the results.

Those who have examined the Book of Genesis have found that there are two creation stories in the early chapters. The first of these is attributed to a writer or group of writers called "P" because of the priestly character of what they wrote. The second creation story, which begins in the middle of Genesis 2:4, is attributed to a writer called "J" who wrote five centuries earlier than P. He is called J because of his preference for the name Jahveh or Yahweh when referring to God. In the Revised Standard Version this name is printed in capitals, LORD. Notice that it is not used in the first chapter but occurs several times in chapters 2—4.[1]

The P Account of Creation

The priestly writer conceived the earth as a flat surface over which the "firmament" arched like an upturned bowl. To the inside of this bowl are fastened the sun, moon, and stars. There are waters above the firmament which fall down through "the windows of heaven" when God opens them and there is rain (Gen. 1: 6-7; 7:11; 8:2). There is also water under the earth, as anyone knows who has used a well. When there is a big flood, water seems to come out of the ground, from the "fountains of the deep," as well as from the sky (Gen. 8:2). Thus the world as conceived by P may be drawn like this:

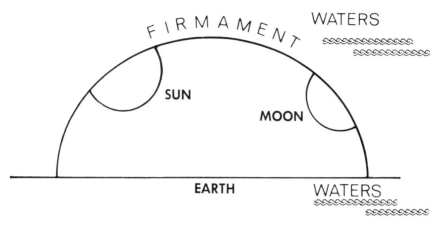

For the P writer, God created the world amid the waters of chaos as a man might make a clearing in the jungle on which to live and plant crops. In the midst of the primeval chaos, God created order and life. He placed barriers against the disorder and death which are symbolized by darkness and the surging waters above and beneath the earth. But the chaos is not destroyed, just as the jungle continues to surround the clearing. When light departs and night falls, chaos takes over temporarily. Creation is renewed each morning with the return of light. When there is a great flood, man's life and work are endangered by the threatening waters. Only the power and promise of God protects him from being overwhelmed (Gen 8:21-22).

When we compare Genesis 1 with other ancient creation accounts found in the Near East, we notice immediately how majestic God appears in the biblical version. There is no struggle among the gods as in some of the other stories. The world does not proceed out of God. In fact, he is completely separated from the world which he creates. And there is only one God. He simply speaks, and light is created. In an orderly way, with deliberate speed, he makes the firmament, the seas, the dry land, plants, animals, and man. He rules all of his creation, including the stars. These were regarded in the ancient world as living forces which could bring good or evil to mankind. We pay homage to this old belief whenever we turn to the horoscope in our daily paper. But for the P writer in Genesis, the stars are insignificant and are under God's rule. They merit only two words in the original Hebrew of Genesis 1:16.

The world which God created is good. This belief is repeated again and again in Genesis 1. Even the great sea monsters, which seem to serve no useful purpose, are regarded as good (1:21). The sun and moon were created by God in order to give mankind a calendar. It is important to know when to plant crops and when to observe the great religious festivals. This need is supplied by the lights which God placed in the heavens and which man uses to determine the seasons (1:14). In fact, everything that God made has worth and purpose. Genesis 3 tells how the world went wrong and why there is trouble in it. But Genesis 1 affirms that it was not so in the original intent of God. All that God made was good.

The most startling statement in Genesis 1 is not the assertion that the world was created in six days. We find it even harder to believe that all God's work is good. We deny this whenever we become discouraged and whenever we feel that the cards are stacked against us. We need to hear again the great affirmation of faith expressed by the P writer in Genesis 1. We need to rediscover the basic intent of God in making the world and putting us into it. We need to conform ourselves to the good purposes of God so that the trust and hope expressed in this chapter may be vindicated.

The culmination of Genesis 1 is the creation of mankind (vss. 26-28). Why does God say, "Let *us* make man . . ."? The word for God in Hebrew is plural, perhaps because he is so much greater than any individual. The plural here is one of majesty rather than of number. This may explain why God uses the plural pronoun in referring to himself. Or it may be that the writer is thinking of God's addressing the heavenly beings which surround him and do his bidding.

What is meant by the image of God? In what way is man like God? Much has been written about this, and no final answer can be given. Man is like God in that he has a large amount of freedom to decide his own destiny. Man participates in God's act of creation by growing plants and inventing tools. Man is like God in that he walks upright and looks to the heavens, where God is believed to dwell. In any event, there is a kinship between God and man which sets man off from all other creatures. God is able to talk with persons and be understood. Man hears God and responds to him.

Man is created male and female (vs. 27). Mankind is incomplete unless both sexes are included on an equal basis. It is important to note that man is made in God's image only in this dual character. This can only mean that God also participates in the dual, male-and-female nature of mankind. We do violence to both man and God when we emphasize only the male side of the duality. When we speak of God as "he," let us make a mental note that the term includes both male and female aspects of God.

Man is given dominion over the fish, the birds, the cattle, and all living things (vs. 26). Does this mean that we can do anything we choose with the earth and its resources? Such an interpretation goes against the whole tenor of the biblical message. The prophets condemned those who hoarded the fruits of the earth and refused to share them with the widows and the fatherless. Jesus scorned the rich man who gathered his goods into barns and allowed his soul to perish. The Bible as a whole teaches our responsibility to use what God has given for human welfare and to guard it against waste and abuse.

On the seventh day, God finished his work and rested (Gen. 2:2-3). This feature of the priestly creation story justified and explained the weekly observance of the sabbath. It also tied the creation of the world to the ritual acts of man, which go on continually. By refraining from work one day and reverently turning to God in prayer, the Jewish worshiper acknowledged his dependence on the Holy One. By taking up his work again on the day after the sabbath, the Jew participated in God's creative work. He affirmed that God's world is good, and he willingly took his place within it. Thus the creation story was not simply an account of what happened long ago but a confession of faith about who God is, what the world is, and what man's place is in the world. It is a statement which has continuing relevance, one which we do well to study and follow even today.

The J Account of Creation

Beginning in the middle of Genesis 2:4 is quite a different version of the creation. In this account, attributed to a writer called J, man is created before the plants and animals. He is male only, not male and female, and woman appears almost as an afterthought. Nothing is said about light, the heavenly bodies, or the sabbath, so prominent in Genesis 1. The J account of creation seems to have a distinct approach and a different concern. It tells of the origin of the names of animals, the basis of marriage, and the answers to such questions as: How did sin begin? Why is there enmity between the serpent and man? Why does the serpent crawl on its belly? Why does woman have pain in childbirth? Why do men toil in earning a living? The writer assumes that there are answers to these questions and he proceeds to give them. The result is a very naive and childlike account of what must have happened when the world was young.

Most striking is the different picture of God found in Genesis 2—3). God is here called the LORD or Yahweh, using the special name of Israel's deity. (The writer of Genesis 1 did not use this, probably because he felt it was inappropriate before the name was revealed to Moses, Exodus 3:13-15.) Instead of creating simply by means of the spoken word, the LORD God formed man from the dust, much as a potter makes an urn from a lump of clay. God did not say, "Let the earth bring forth vegetation" (1:11) but planted a garden like any other farmer (2:8). In Genesis 2, the creation takes place in a somewhat haphazard, trial-and-error fashion. God makes man and then plants a garden in which to place him. He discovers that man is lonely and makes the animals to be his companions. When this does not satisfy man, God seems perplexed about what to do. At last the solution dawns upon him, and he makes woman! Like a wealthy planter out walking among his crops, God visits the garden in the cool of the declining sun (3:8). He calls for the man, not knowing where the man is. Suspicious because the man is hiding, God asks what he has done. The man and woman have to tell God what has taken place during God's absence.

These two different pictures of God recur throughout the Bible. God is both transcendent (far above man) and immanent (involved in the life of man).

For thus says the high and lofty One
    who inhabits eternity, whose name is Holy:
"I dwell in the high and holy place,
    and also with him who is of a contrite
        and humble spirit,
to revive the spirit of the humble,
    and to revive the heart of the contrite.
—Isa. 57:15
	God is transcendent,
	as in Genesis 1.
	
	God is immanent,
	as in Genesis 2—3.

Genesis 1 shows us a God who is all-wise and all-powerful, but there is a coldness and remoteness about him. He seems like an astronomer or a mathematician, dispassionately viewing the order and structure of his universe. The LORD God in Genesis 2—3, however, is warm and approachable, at least until the man and woman disobey him. In a sense, God is made in man's image in the J story of creation. He forms man with his own hands and breathes his own breath into the body of man. He touches human life in an intimate way. He is subject to some of the same limitations which we know. This conception of God is about five hundred years older than the one found in Genesis 1. In many ways it seems primitive and incomplete. But it provides a needed emphasis on the closeness of God to human life. In the same way, the Gospel of John speaks of the exalted Word which is the agent of creation and then says that he became flesh and dwelt among us (1:1-5, 11). God is both far above us and also intimately related to us. To emphasize either of these conceptions of God at the expense of the other is not biblical.

What is woman's natural place? What are her rights? Almost all of us have some answers to these questions, but few of us can give reasons for our conclusions. We have strong feelings about what women are and should be, feelings which may not bear close or critical examination.

What did the J writer say about the place of woman? She was made from Adam's rib, which may suggest to some readers that she was and is inferior to man. She was made after man to serve the need of man. We are not told that God breathed into woman, as he did into the man. According to J, woman bears at least part of the blame for the first sin, disobeying God's command not to eat of the tree of knowledge.

But this is not the whole story of woman in J. She has a more important place than these statements would indicate. Living in a patriarchal society where servant girls and even wives were regarded as the mere instruments of men, the J writer gave woman an important role. There was only one woman in the life of the original man. Monogamy was the pattern long before it became common. God created the woman because he perceived a need in man's life which the animals could not supply. She was not made as a mother, a baby machine, but as a fit companion for man. God created woman out of man's rib, indicating both a closeness and a separateness in their relationship. Something of the physical sensation of yearning for the opposite sex is expressed in this story of woman's creation from man's body. What has been separated must come back together again.

God brought the woman to man to see how he would react to her and what he would call her. There is playfulness in this account. The LORD God seems to enjoy the game of experiment and discovery with the creatures he has made. There is here a profound understanding and appreciation of sexual intercourse. It is not simply a means of relieving tension, as it almost became for the apostle Paul centuries later (1 Cor. 7:9), but an experience of communion between two persons who are made for each other and who need each other deeply.

Jesus accepted the insights of Genesis concerning the correct relationship between men and women (Matt. 19:3-9). God has made them for each other. In marriage they leave their parents and cleave to each other, becoming one flesh. Jesus added, "What therefore God has joined together, let no man put asunder." In its time, this was a powerful assertion of the rights of women, for a man could easily dismiss his wife in biblical society. Jesus sought

29

to protect women from arbitrary treatment and to show that they are persons, to be encountered in a meaningful and lasting relationship, not mere objects to be used and then cast aside. Jesus drew his understanding of marriage from the J writer, who a thousand years before had given woman a relatively high place in relation to man.

The Nature and Origin of Sin

During my college days, I frequently hitched a ride between home and school. Once I caught a ride with a truck driver who wanted to discuss (what else?) theology and ethics. He was fascinated with the story of Adam and Eve. It was his impression that sin is basically sexual indulgence and that it all began with a perverse and foolish woman in the Garden of Eden. This was a mistaken view, but such ideas have been expressed by others who should have known better. Genesis 3 has been the occasion for countless ideas and beliefs, many of which have little support in the original text. It has furnished material to preachers, theologians, artists, playwrights, and poets through the centuries. Augustine of Hippo, John Calvin, Reinhold Niebuhr, John Milton, and Arthur Miller are only a few of those who have meditated on the meaning of these verses in Genesis. Such great interest in the Garden of Eden is due to the interesting way in which the story is told and to the vital questions of life which are addressed in it.

Several important ideas are expressed or implied in Genesis 3. First, human beings are free to make many important decisions. This is by no means obvious to everybody today. An important school of psychology holds that our freedom is only an illusion, that we simply respond to rewards and punishments as a machine responds to electrical impulses. Many individuals feel helpless, unable to control their own destinies. Do we believe that we can explore the possibilities open to us, decide which is best, and then act on our decision? Whenever we decide that it is time for us to change our ways of living, can we do so? Genesis 3 suggests that some real choices are open to us. God told the first couple that they could taste all of the fruits of the garden. Only one tree was forbidden, and they were even free to choose it—and then suffer the consequences of their action!

Sin is seen as disobedience in Genesis. The man and the woman ate of the tree which God had told them not to touch. They did not break a rule or a law written in a book somewhere. They did something which God had forbidden. Thus sin is not the technical violation of an abstract rule but the breakdown of a personal relationship. It begins with estrangement from God and disobedience, and it results in even further estrangement. Part of the beauty of life in the garden before this happened was the free and open relationship which the two people enjoyed in the presence of God. When they disregarded his instructions, this came to an end. There are in our own experience several different kinds and degrees of wrongdoing. One of the most tragic is the sin in which we deliberately turn our backs on God.

A subtle but important point is that sin is a matter of the mind, not of the body. Our bodies, like all that God has made, are neutral. They may be used for good or for evil, as we choose. Eve was not dragged down by the passions of her flesh, compelled to sin by an uncontrollable lust. She made a deliberate choice on the basis of a rational examination of the situation. She was not hungry, but she was curious about that strange fruit! She was betrayed by the highest part of her nature, her mind. Sexual indulgence is not mentioned and probably has little to do with Genesis 3. Sexual intercourse is part of God's creation and plan. The act itself is not condemned anywhere in the Bible. This is a misconception of puritanical Christians. What the Bible does condemn is the abuse of sex or of any other gift of God. When the gift of sex is used in ways which degrade ourselves or other persons, instead of making possible the personal fulfillment which God intended in giving us this potential, we have sinned against God's law. But this is not to be blamed on the passions of the body. Like the choice of Eve, it is a decision we make with our minds.

The basic sin of Adam and Eve was pride, not sensual indulgence. They refused to accept the command and warning of God. They believed the serpent's suggestion that eating the forbidden fruit would make them like God (3:5). It was their ambition which led the man and woman to disobey the rules and to lose their innocence. They wanted to have something which God had not given, even though they already had plenty. They wanted to be something which God had not intended for them to be. The greatest sins in our own day may not be the crimes of anger and lust, harmful as these certainly can be. The greatest sins may be the polite, legal, "acceptable" sins of respectable and reasonable persons who aim for power, money, and prestige and will do whatever is necessary to get them.

Much has been written about the significance of the serpent. We should avoid reading too much into the text. We are not told that the serpent is really the devil. Perhaps it is nothing more than a talking snake. But it does suggest that there is something insidious about sin. We do not simply stumble into wrongdoing in the same way we might stumble over a step in the dark. Sin has a way of coming to us before we even think of going to it. It insinuates itself into our thinking. It convinces us that good is evil and that evil is good. It persuades us to do wrong by distorting the choices open to us and by lying to us about their consequences. We need to be on guard against sin, lest it should weaken our defenses and captivate our minds. It is busy at the work of corrupting us. If we do not realize this and take the necessary precautions, we will suffer.

Another important implication of Genesis 3 is that knowledge is not a guarantee against sin. We often act on the assumption that our personal and social problems can be solved by education. Smoking is harmful to health. Tell smokers this, and they will stop. Right? Wrong. Knowing what is harmful does not make us avoid it. Knowing what is good for us does not make us choose what is good. Knowledge does not solve our human predicament. Eve had been told not to eat the apple, but she did it nevertheless. Her knowledge was quickly overcome by the falsehoods of the serpent. Even then she used her own cleverness to try to evade the consequences and the guilt for what she had done. The more we know, the more we use our knowledge to distort and attempt to escape the truth. Sometimes those who have had little experience in life are wiser than persons with long training who will not follow the clear directions implied by the facts. "A little child shall lead them" (Isa. 11:6).

Paul later carried the concept of our helplessness in the presence of sin to even greater lengths. In the Letter to the Romans, he wrote: "I can will what is right, but I cannot do it. For I do not do the good I want, but the evil I do not want is what I do" (7:18-19). It does no good to preach to a person who is having such an experience. It would do such a person no good to take a course on ethics or to make New Year resolutions. He or she can overcome sin only when given special power from God. According to Paul, sin holds us in an unbreakable grip until a greater force overcomes it. Genesis 3 does not paint sin in such dark colors, to be sure, but it already recognizes that human cleverness is not able to deal with the persuasiveness of sin.

Genesis 3 sees the original human condition as one of innocence. We were not cruel savages who became civilized and restrained. As we grew in knowledge and ability, we became more corrupt, not less. "Progress" is not necessarily a blessing. Things were in some ways better when we were children, when we did not know as much. Even knowledge of good and evil is not an unmixed blessing. Notice that such knowledge does not lead Adam and Eve to do right. It comes to them only after they have done wrong, and even then it does not guarantee right behavior. The J writer, who told this story, was basically skeptical about human progress and doubtful about how well we can understand and overcome our problems. The fact that we have used our knowledge of physics to make hydrogen bombs and that we have polluted our air and water would come as no surprise to him.

The participants in the sin described in Genesis 3 are punished. The serpent is compelled to crawl, the woman to have pain in childbirth, and the man to toil as he works. There is a seriousness about sin here and throughout the Bible. The consequences of deliberate disobedience may not be evaded. Jesus stressed this again and again. If we build our house upon shifting sand, he said, the house will fall. (Matt. 7:24-27.) If we do what is wrong, what God forbids, we will bring harm to ourselves and perhaps to others as well.

All of the above ideas are, I believe, implied in Genesis 3. One important idea which is suggested but not sufficiently stressed in this chapter is the grace of God toward sinners. God made Adam and Eve and gave them the blessings of life. He offered them everything they needed. He endowed them with freedom of choice. Even when they disobeyed him, he did not turn away from them completely. He made garments for them, in order to cover their nakedness revealed by their sin (3:21). He enabled Eve to bear other children (4:1). The remainder of the Bible gives many examples of the grace and love of God. He forgives our sin and calls us back to a satisfying and life-giving relationship with him. Jesus dramatized this truth in the parable of the prodigal son. We should not read the description of sin in Genesis 3 without recalling the fact that God makes it possible for us to return to him. Much of the rest of the Bible was written to emphasize that fact.

Some Reflections on Genesis 1—3

How did two creation stories, so different from each other, come to stand side by side in our Bible? The editor who placed them together must have understood the differences in sequence, in the understanding of God, and in the goodness of creation expressed by the two accounts. It seems to me that the editor deliberately placed the two divergent stories next to each other. Together they now form such a natural whole that the casual reader does not notice the break between them. The first story is orderly; the second is disorderly and random. The first story shows God as a careful planner. The second shows him as a playful, childlike, experimenter. The first story affirms that the world has purpose and that it is basically good. The second story realistically probes the

33

ways in which the world and man have been corrupted. It recognizes the obvious fact that there is much wrong with the world as we experience it. Together the two stories of creation express both pessimism and optimism—pessimism about life as it is and optimism about life as it can be. There is frank appraisal of the human predicament with no effort to gloss over the real evil and sin which we all experience. On the other hand, there is a bold affirmation of the fundamental rightness of all that God has made, an affirmation which holds out hope for those who would seek to recover and restore mankind to its original freedom and dignity.

These creation accounts do not tell us what happened a long time ago. They have little if any scientific or historical value. But they do tell us something about right now. They tell us who we are and what we can be. They explore our relationship to each other and to God. They tell us about the world of nature and our relationship to it. They tell us where we may have gone wrong and suggest some ways in which we may get back to the right path. Thus it is correct to stress the religious value of Genesis 1—3. But even the religious value of these chapters needs to be qualified. Too little is said here about the real power we have to deal with evil forces outside us and within us. Too little stress is given to God's mercy and forgiveness in these chapters. Too little is said about the ways in which God reaches out for us in order to restore us to him. This is why Genesis 1—3 needs to be placed within the whole sweep of biblical revelation. We need to read these chapters with the message of the Gospels in mind. They are insufficient and misleading by themselves.

The whole message of the Bible cannot be stated in a few sentences or chapters. In fact, the message of God cannot be expressed in words alone. There must be experience which confirms the words in order to make them real for us. It took a thousand years of suffering and joy, despair and hope, for the people of Israel and the followers of Christ to receive and record the message of the Bible. The words of the prophets, the events of Israel's history, the coming of Jesus, the founding of the church—all these are part of the message of God in scripture. It is not surprising, then, that these creation stories in Genesis need to be supplemented. They become meaningful to us only when we see them as part of the whole sweep of God's self-revealing in the Bible. Understood against such a background, they express eloquently a fundamental conviction that the world is good and that it is ruled by a loving and purposeful God.

34

Chapter 3

The Prophets
as Persons

Jesus loved and made use of the books of the prophets. When asked to read in his home synagogue at Nazareth, he selected a passage from the Book of Isaiah. Even when he did not quote them directly, Jesus used the prophets as a guide for his life and for his teachings. It is reported that some people even thought Jesus was one of the prophets come back to life (Matt. 16:14).

We would like to read and to understand the prophets, but there are barriers which keep us from doing so. We easily recall stories about Joseph, David, and other Old Testament heroes, but few of us know much about Jeremiah and Ezekiel. What we know about these men does not encourage us to know more. We may think of them as strange, hostile, and forbidding. When we open their books, we read about strange visions—whirling wheels and boiling pots. Without guidance it is difficult to decide what the prophets are talking about. Philip found an Ethiopian official puzzling over some verses in Isaiah and asked, "Do you understand what you are reading?" The Ethiopian replied, "How can I, unless someone guides me?" (Acts 8:30-31).

In this chapter I want to convey some of my enthusiasm about the prophets in general, give a profile of Amos and Hosea, and suggest how you may learn more about these and other prophets.

Amos' Concern for the Welfare of Persons

Turn, in your Bible, to the first and second chapters of Amos. Here is a sermon which shows us the central concerns of the prophet. He who spoke these words was a careful observer of the events of his time. He was well acquainted with the nations and peoples who lived in his part of the world. Without benefit of newspapers or television, he knew what was happening in many places. Amos was a shepherd and a farmer in the hill country of Judah, not far from Bethlehem, where shepherds are still to be seen. He must have visited Jerusalem, Samaria, and other cities as well as the market town of Bethel, where he preached to the crowds. Here he could have talked with merchants and travelers who had visited distant places. Amos was concerned about history and current events because he believed that God is intimately involved in such events. What has happened in the past reveals what God has done and what he is. What will happen in the future depends on the decision of God. While many persons in the time of Amos believed that each nation had its own god, Amos assumed that Yahweh, the God of Israel and Judah, was Lord of the other nations as well. This farmer from the hills of Judah had a universal vision and a profound faith!

In the name of God, Amos condemned the sins of eight nations in chapters 1 and 2. Notice where these are located on the map shown here. Amos came from Tekoa in Judah, and he preached at Bethel in Israel. We can imagine his listeners paying close attention as he deplored the sins of the surrounding peoples, becoming somewhat uneasy as he spoke of neighboring Judah, and then exploding in anger when he began to list their own shortcomings. At first glance, the sermon seems cruel and bitter. It tells of the terrible vengeance which God will bring upon many nations. There is little hope or encouragement in these chapters.

And yet the sermon has a compassionate side. It is filled with indignation about what has happened to human beings. What Amos condemns is the way in which persons have been shoved around by military and political leaders. The residents of Gilead were threshed with iron sledges (1:3). Gaza took a whole people into slavery (1:6). In a similar way, Tyre broke a sacred covenant (1:9). The pitiless cruelty of Edom is described (1:11). The Ammonites carried on a war in which they ripped up pregnant women "that they might enlarge their border" (1:13). Amos cared little for "national security" or "military necessity." He could see no reason for the way in which persons had been treated by the nations in his region. He could accept no argument to justi-

Places Mentioned by Amos in Chapters 1 and 2

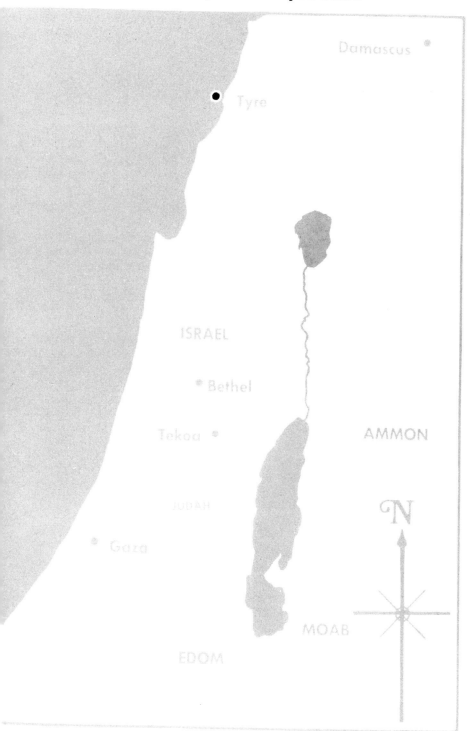

fy all the bloodshed. In the eyes of God, he claimed, people are of paramount importance. No one can ride over them roughshod without being held accountable to Yahweh.

A few years ago I spoke about this chapter to a class of young adults. I carefully avoided saying anything about what the chapter meant in contemporary terms. When I had finished, one of the students smiled and said, "I came here to learn about the Bible, but you insist on talking about Vietnam!"

Most of us recall what happened in that country with regret. But few of us really sense the nature and scope of the tragedy. We speak of our errors of judgment—it was the wrong war in the wrong place—but not of our basically perverted aims and attitudes. We speak of some fifty thousand American lives lost, but we rarely think of the millions of Vietnamese casualties. Amos was concerned about the people of other nations, many of which had been enemies of his people for centuries! In the name of God he condemned those who would mistreat such persons. No human being is worthy of death, he contended, simply because he happens to live in a different territory or happens to get into the path of our armies. The God of Amos did not lead his people in righteous crusades against those who threatened world freedom. This God brings punishment to all, including his own people, who in their thirst for power callously disregard the welfare of others.

I have the feeling that we ourselves have quite a way to go in order to catch up with the thinking of this man who lived twenty-seven centuries ago. This is why I have difficulty with the phrase "progressive revelation." It implies that the early writers of the Bible did not know as much about God and his will as the later writers did. But here in Amos, the earliest prophet for whom we have a book, we find a universal vision and a broad sympathy which is very close to the teaching of Jesus and of Paul. There were others who came after Amos, such as Ezra and Nehemiah, who did not have the same breadth and compassion. We cannot neatly divide the writings of the Bible into those which are early and therefore incomplete, on the one hand, and those which are late and therefore complete, on the other. Some of the persons who wrote, and were written about, understood God better than others did, but some of the wisest were also the earliest.

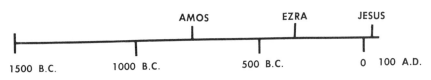

Amos' Preaching About Social Justice

The prophet Amos was not only concerned about what happened to persons in distant nations, but he also called for more compassion toward those who suffered among his own people. He came from Judah, one of the two kingdoms into which the domain of David and Solomon was divided after the death of the latter, two centuries before Amos. He preached in Bethel, a market town and shrine in the sister nation of Israel. At this time, Israel had just completed a war with Damascus in which a large chunk of territory had been won. This brought prosperity to some persons and inflation to all. Those who already had plenty used their power to gain more. The poor and helpless, especially orphans and widows, lost what little they had. Many went into debt or were sold into slavery.

Amos was filled with outrage toward some who were wealthy and smug. He said that they lay on beds of ivory, a luxury item, and stretched on couches. They idly strummed on musical instruments and even composed songs, while all about them others were struggling to survive (6:4-7). The prophet condemned those businessmen who were so impatient to make money that they could not wait until religious holidays were over. They manipulated grain sales in order to enrich themselves and impoverish their customers. Amos said they "buy the poor for silver and the needy for a pair of sandals" (8:4-6). He condemned the wealthy women of Samaria, whom he called "Cows of Bashan." Demanding a higher and higher standard of living, they compelled their husbands to satisfy their inordinate appetites by robbing and oppressing the poor (4:1). While Amos had great compassion for persons who suffered, there were others whose attitudes and behavior he could not tolerate!

Amos clearly valued people and their needs more than he did property and its prerogatives. He was not a cloistered saint who preached withdrawal from the world. He recognized that people must live by labor and the exchange of goods, but he deplored the manipulation of the market which results in injury to persons. He criticized the wasteful expenditures of the rich, especially when coupled with unconcern about other persons and even with a willingness to cheat (8:5). Amos did not believe that property rights come first. When property is used to destroy human beings, or when it is placed before the needs of persons, its owners must be held responsible. The rich are not free to use what they have in a way that causes others to go hungry or to perish.

Amos spoke often about justice and righteousness. The first word comes from the Hebrew root meaning "to judge." A judge was one who corrected imbalances and set things straight. Often this meant shielding the poor and helpless against the depradations of the rich and powerful. Justice in Israel was not blind, but it was aware of and sensitive to the hurts of persons. Justice did not mean giving every person exactly what he or she had earned or deserved. In effect, it meant being partial toward those in greatest need. Righteousness meant more than simply obeying laws, whether made by man or given by God. It meant being kind and considerate toward persons in need. Justice and righteousness are the attributes of a kind and merciful God, one who cares about what happens to persons and restores them to happiness and strength. A community which establishes justice and righteousness is one which fulfills these great purposes of God.

What would Amos say about some of the things that happen in our communities today? What would he say about the ways in which we spend our money? What market practices would draw his fire? What would he suggest that we should do in order to establish justice?

Here are some statements sometimes heard today. Think about what Amos would say about them:

He was born of poor but honest parents (suggesting that poor people aren't usually honest).

Elder So-and-so is an important man (meaning well-to-do).

The national budget will have to be cut. Let's take out unnecessary expenses like Aid to Dependent Children.

If you try hard enough in this country, you'll succeed. (If I don't succeed, what does that say about me?)

The church should not try to tell a corporation how to manage its affairs.

Amos and the People of God

In the 1950s we added the phrase "under God" to the Pledge of Allegiance. What does it mean to be a nation under God? For Amos it was not a very comfortable place to be! In one of his sermons, he told the people that God cared for them more than for any other group:

> You only have I known
> of all the families of the earth. . . .

There was nothing new about this idea. It was what everyone in Israel assumed. God had chosen them, they believed, and would bless them with peace and security. He would protect them from their enemies, and if war should come would assure them victory. But this was not the conclusion which Amos drew from the first proposition:

> You only have I known
> of all the families of the earth;
> therefore I will punish you
> for all your iniquities. (3:2)

Those who are chosen by God are held especially responsible by God. Those who receive great gifts are expected to fulfill important tasks. Those who fail to do what God requires, especially those who are his friends and should know his will, are to receive punishment for their neglect.

In a vision, Amos saw Yahweh holding a plumb line against a wall, like a bricklayer testing his work. Yahweh told him that he was also measuring his people with a plumb line. Because they were out of alignment, they would be torn down and punished (7:7-9). This was startling and disturbing news to the people of Israel, who regarded themselves as under Yahweh's special protection. Sometimes Amos seemed to agree with their sense of being specially called by God, but for him it meant responsibility as well as privilege. He also insisted that God had blessed other nations besides Israel. To be sure, he had led the Israelites out of Egypt, but he had also led other nations into new lands (9:7). Thus Amos undermined the exclusiveness and pretentiousness of his people's religious creed.

Amos had some bitter things to say about worship as he observed it in the shrine cities of Bethel and Gilgal:

> Come to Bethel and transgress;
> to Gilgal, and multiply transgression . . . (4:4)

It was like saying, "Come to church and sin!" Worship was sinful in Israel because it was used to cover up wrongdoing and neglect of persons. Worship is futile and even blasphemous when it lulls us into the feeling that we are on good terms with God when we are not. It is a sham when it conceals greed and cruelty. It is useless when it is substituted for genuine compassion and action on behalf of those in need.

Amos pictures God rejecting those who come to his house to offer gifts and to carry out elaborate acts of worship:

> I hate, I despise your feasts,
> and I take no delight in your solemn assemblies . . .
> Take away from me the noise of your songs;
> to the melody of your harps I will listen.
> But let justice roll down like waters,
> and righteousness like an everflowing stream. (5:21-24)

It is sometimes said that the church should concern itself with spiritual affairs, such as evangelism and worship, and not meddle

41

in social issues or political matters. But if the church shows no concern for measures which affect the welfare of persons, even its worship and evangelism are unacceptable to God.

The Prophet Meets the Priest

Amos 7:10-17 describes an interesting encounter between two religious leaders. Though both of them served Yahweh, it would be hard to imagine two persons more unlike in aims and attitudes. Amaziah was a political appointee, sent to supervise worship in the government sanctuary at Bethel. To keep his people from crossing the border to worship in Jerusalem after his country separated from Judah, King Jeroboam I established Bethel and other places for their worship. Thus the place and its services were instruments of national policy.

Amaziah fitted neatly into this pattern, drawing his salary and upholding the established order. When he heard about Amos' preaching, he sent word to the king accusing the prophet of conspiracy against the nation. The prophet had said that the king would die and the people be carried into exile. Like others in his day, Amaziah took the spoken word much more seriously than we do. He believed that what prophets like Amos say have a tendency to come true, simply because the words have been spoken. Therefore it is imperative to silence the prophet who speaks words of doom, for "the land is not able to bear all his words."

Amaziah tried to persuade Amos to go back to his native Judah and there "eat bread." He suggested that the prophet might earn his living just as well or better among his own people. He assumed that Amos was in the prophecy business for what he could make from it. He also told Amos that Bethel was a royal chapel and ought not to be subjected to the kind of harsh sermons Amos generated. It seemed a little like discussing our national priorities at a White House prayer breakfast. At the very least it was rude, and it might even border on treason.

Amos retorted that he was not a prophet at all. The profession had received a bad name, and reading the Old Testament we can understand why. Many prophets did try to make a profit from their work. Many said what their listeners wanted them to say. Prophets were paid by kings with the understanding that they would only foretell good things. Amos did not want to be associated with such frauds. He said that he had been minding his own business when God took him from behind the flock and compelled him to go and preach. He could not disobey God in order to satisfy Amaziah's request. Here were two religious leaders who could not agree on what God required of them. One represented a church which sustains the status quo and upholds the state. The other spoke of a faith which shakes the whole foundations of society.

Because Amos rejected false worship and concerned himself with the needs of persons, one might suppose that he had little spiritual depth. But Amos had an exalted view of God as the Creator and Sustainer of all things. The LORD of hosts "forms the mountains, and creates the wind, and declares to man what is his thought" (4:13). He "turns deep darkness into the morning, and darkens the day into night." He "calls for the waters of the sea, and pours them out upon the surface of the earth" (5:8). Amos repeatedly called on persons to seek this majestic God and to find life in him. Amos has been called a prophet of doom. Compared with other prophets, he appears negative and lacking in hope. He ridiculed those who longed for the Day of the LORD because it would be a time of destruction, not of glory (5:18-20). Yet there are places in the book where a glimmer of light breaks through:

> Seek good, and not evil,
>   that you may live;
> and so the LORD, the God of hosts, will be with you,
>   as you have said.
> Hate evil, and love good,
>   and establish justice in the gate;
> It may be that the LORD, the God of hosts,
>   will be gracious to the remnant of Joseph. (5:14-15)

Hosea's Domestic Tragedy

George Adam Smith, the noted Bible interpreter, wrote that "a prophet is a life behind a voice." Prophets do not simply parrot some words or pass on a message without becoming personally involved in what they are saying. A secretary can sometimes transcribe a letter without knowing or caring what it contains, but a prophet cannot treat a sermon in this way. Thus Isaiah gave his children names that corresponded to his sermons—"Speedy Booty, Speedy Prey" and "A Remnant Shall Return." Jeremiah was so profoundly moved by his message of woe that it nearly tore him apart. And Hosea's intimate family experiences became so interlaced with his proclamation that it is difficult now to separate the two. We cannot be sure when he is giving God's message, when he is describing his own tragedy, and when he is doing both.

Many scholars have attempted to reconstruct the events of Hosea's marriages from the few hints that are found in the Book of Hosea. There is much disagreement about this, and it is hard to decide which explanation is correct. What is offered here is one plausible version, and I recognize that it is not at all certain.

Hosea understood what love and marriage ought to be and could be. When they were young together, he and Gomer had enjoyed a rich and satisfying relationship. He had brought her gifts as a sign of his devotion and had whispered tenderly about his feelings for her. It is only when we assume such early joy that we can explain Hosea's insight into the romance of God with his people (Hosea 2:14f).

Children were born to the marriage, and Hosea named the first one *Jezreel*. Jezreel was a place where something notorious had happened, and Hosea had a message regarding it. Everyone knew what was meant by the word, just as we know what is meant by "Kent State." So Hosea's first child was a kind of walking sermon to remind people of his father's views.

The second child was called *Lo-Ruchamah*, "She Who Is Without Compassion" or "She Who Receives No Compassion." The word comes from a Hebrew root meaning "womb." I like to think that it refers to the kind of tender affection which a pregnant woman feels for her unborn child. There was not much love in Hosea's house when the second child was born. A man once came to me for help because his marriage was deteriorating. "When I come home from work," he said, "I get more affection from the dog than I get from my wife." Something like that happened to Hosea and Gomer, and the change is reflected in the second child's name.

Gomer had strange hungers. One man was not enough for her. She longed for other lovers, and she gave herself to them. Hosea had confirmed his suspicions by the time the third child was born. He named this one *Lo-Ammi*, "Not My People" or "Not Mine." For a time he held the vain hope that the marriage might be saved. He stifled his indignation and tried to smooth things over. He even tried to use the children to persuade Gomer, knowing that his own appeals to her were useless:

> "Plead with your mother, plead—
>   for she is not my wife,
>   and I am not her husband—
> that she put away her harlotry from her face,
>   and her adultery from between her breasts. (2:2)

What Hosea Learned

But Hosea must have known that the children could not restore the broken relationship. Gomer left, and Hosea was alone with his thoughts. He recalled the tender joy with which they had once approached each other, the spoken and unspoken commitments that they had exchanged. He recalled the gifts that he had offered to Gomer, and he did not regret these because they had expressed something deeply felt. What disturbed him was the way in which his generosity had not been repaid with contempt. Shattered agreements and flaunted vows were strewn along the length of their path together. Gomer had become a stranger to him. A seemingly insatiable appetite had seized her and had made of her a hard, uncommunicative, baffling creature.

Did Hosea know from the first that Gomer would turn out like this? He suggests that this was the case (1:2). But here Hosea looks at the past through tear-filled eyes. He reads back into the past the emotions of the present. If Hosea knew all along about Gomer's weakness, then the whole book becomes a charade. In fact, it appears that Hosea loved Gomer at first with all the sincerity and innocence of one who expected nothing but joy in his marriage. Only thus can we explain the disappointment and bitterness that swept over his soul when he learned the truth.

Then Hosea thought long, as he reflected on the loss of Gomer, about the relationship between God and the people of Israel. He had called them out of Egypt into a kind of marriage, just as Hosea had once taken Gomer from her father's house and had created a new life with her. God had given his people a rich and productive land as a wedding present. Hosea spoke lovingly of the land, as one who loves birds and fields and rain and sunshine. But in this new land the people had turned away from Yahweh and had worshiped alien gods, nature deities, in the hope of gaining better crops and richer gifts. They had engaged in the fertility cults, having intercourse with prostitutes at every shrine. In short, they had forsaken their first husband and had committed adultery with others, just as Gomer had done. Hosea now understood what God had felt in his encounter with Israel because he himself had gone through the same loss!

Hosea learned something about the nature of sin. For Amos, who had preached a few years earlier, sin was something you might have done last Tuesday. It was something specific. It was weighing your thumb with the merchandise or not giving the correct change. But for Hosea, sin was more than breaking a rule. It was not something that you do but something that you are or something you become. It was not an act but an attitude. It was all the hardness and alienation that he saw in the face of Gomer, her eyes averted and her lips pursed. Sin for Hosea was turning away from the One who loves you and offers himself to you.

Hosea said that there was no knowledge of God among the people (4:1). In the language of the Bible, to know someone often means to have sexual intercourse with that person. A friend of mine lived as a child next to an elderly brother and sister, who lived together and sometimes fought and shouted at each other. She would put him down by saying, "You have never known a woman!" When Hosea said that his people had no knowledge of God, he meant that they had broken off that intimate association with Yahweh which characterizes sexual intercourse. The Book of Hosea is an X-rated story. It uses sexual imagery throughout, both to describe sin and to show what our relationship to God ought to be.

When Hosea saw the analogy between his own experience and God's he realized that his family difficulties had been part of God's plan. Only by going through the joy of possession and the pain of loss could he know what the people of Israel had done and what God had lost. There was no short cut to insight, no way he could know without suffering. Jeremiah later picked up the ideas of Hosea and used them in his sermons, but Jeremiah was never married and could not have understood what Hosea enjoyed and then lost. But Hosea knew.

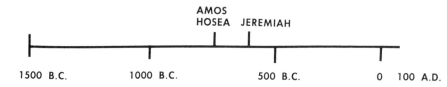

The Restoration of Gomer

Gomer went out in search of a thrill. She found the superficial excitement of sensual indulgence, but she lost forever the deep satisfaction of being with someone who cares and understands. Even the cheap bauble she had gained soon lost its shimmer. She discovered that when she was free to go with any man, few of them wanted her. She was tossed from one to another and then thrown carelessly away. Like many persons who fell into debt in those times, she was offered for sale as a slave. Gomer must have been a pitiful sight as she crouched in the marketplace, for no one would bid for her. And then one bystander placed a bid. It was Hosea ben Beeri! He said that he paid fifteen shekels of silver and a homer and a lecheth of barley—perhaps $120 in today's money. (3:2)

Why did he do it? Was it because there lingered, under all the bitterness and anger and cruel words spoken, a residue of affection? Not a chance! Then why? Hosea did not know—unless this was also part of God's plan, part of the strange curriculum to prepare God's spokesman. Hosea had learned about sin. Now he had to learn about forgiveness and reconciliation.

Forgiveness is not easy to accept. It is painful for the one forgiven because it means admitting that we have been on the wrong course. It requires us to go in a new direction, to tear ourselves from the adulterous relationships to which we have foolishly given ourselves. It means returning and surrendering, with wholeness and integrity, to the One to whom alone our devotion belongs. God does not want our promises, nor even our obedience, unless it is preceded by this kind of self-surrender. A husband once told me that his wife had left home with the children. "I can't understand what she wanted from me," he said, "I gave her everything she could ask. I even took a second job so that I could buy her a car." We discovered later that she had wanted him, not his gifts. God wants us back—not our acts of penance, but ourselves.

Forgiveness is also difficult for the one who forgives. It involves the recollection of old hurts and the risk of new ones. It is costly for God to forgive—expensive in anguish, in uncertainty, in suffering. Hosea saw this and expressed God's distress, being torn between anger and compassion:

> How can I give you up, O Ephraim!
>   How can I hand you over, O Israel!
> My heart recoils within me,
>   my compassion grows warm and tender.
> I will not execute my fierce anger,
>   I will not again destroy Ephraim;
> for I am God and not man,
>   the Holy One in your midst,
>   and I will not come to destroy. (11:8-9)

Hosea recognized that restoration could not come unless God took the initiative. His wayward people could not find their own way back to him. He would have to come to them. He would have to cross the barrier of silence and distrust, a barrier like the one in the prophet's home (3:3). But he knew that God could bridge this opening:

> Therefore, behold, I will allure her,
>   and bring her into the wilderness,
>   and speak tenderly to her.
> And there I will give her her vineyards,
>   and make the Valley of Achor a door of hope.
> And there she shall answer me as in the days of her youth,
>   as at the time when she came out of Egypt. (2:14-15)

And what happened to Hosea and Gomer? Did he allure her and restore the broken relationship? We do not know, for he drew a curtain of privacy across the door of their little home. But there are hints that Hosea had a renaming ceremony of two of the children. "No Compassion" was renamed "Compassion," and "Not Mine" became "Mine" (2:1, 23). Hosea had learned the agony of unrequited love. Had he also learned the meaning of mercy?

Amos and Hosea were similar in some ways and quite different in others. Each of the prophets was an individual, speaking out of unique personal experiences. Each spoke what needed to be said in his particular time—sometimes a word of rebuke, and sometimes a message of encouragement. It is important for us to know something of the prophet and his time in order to grasp the import of his message. What you have learned here about two prophets you can learn elsewhere about the others.[1]

The Remoteness of the Prophets

We can too easily assume that we understand the prophets. We can make them too readily into our own image. Some have seen them primarily as social reformers, but the prophets were not interested in simply abolishing social classes or even in securing justice, apart from a renewed relationship to the God who demands justice. The prophets were concerned about the relationships of persons to one another because they knew that this had everything to do with the relationship between persons and God. They were as much concerned about what happens spiritually to the person who robs as they were about what happens materially to the person who is robbed.

Some have seen the prophets as unwitting predicters of detailed descriptions of events, stored up to be interpreted and used in the tenth century, or the sixteenth, or the twentieth, or whenever the interpreter happens to be alive. But the prophets spoke primarily to their own time and place. It is only when we understand how their words had meaning in their own day that we can see their importance for our time and can hear the distinct word which God would speak to us. The prophet spoke with urgency about matters which his hearers could comprehend and correct, not about remote events which could not interest them at all. The sermons of Amos and Jeremiah are in the imperative, not the indicative, and they call for immediate action.

So there is a great gulf fixed between ourselves and the prophets, a difference in time and temperament, in outlook and purpose. We would probably find Amos to be crude, Ezekiel outlandish. Imagine becoming friendly with Ezekiel, with his months of lying rigid on one side in a kind of hypnotic stupor, his wild dreams, and his ability to see what is happening hundreds of miles away.

It is hard to say at this distance whether any of the prophets were insane, for we cannot even decide what "insanity" is in contemporary subjects. But we must agree that the prophets of the Old Testament walked on a line between normal and abnormal life, between balanced behavior and a kind of holy abandon, and that they sometimes crossed over into an altogether different world from the one we know. To be a prophet one does not have to be crazy, but perhaps it helps to be so.

There is a remoteness about the prophets which is even more significant than their distance from us in social milieu and personal characteristics. It is the difference between what the prophets demanded and what we regard as acceptable behavior. When human beings meet God, Isaiah said, they are aware that they have unclean lips. The prophets were aware of a cleavage between themselves and God, between the content of their message and their own human inclinations, and this is why so many of them were wrenched in the process of speaking for God. One greater than themselves spoke through them, one whose ways were not their ways and whose thoughts were not their thoughts. And so, when we listen to the prophets today, we may expect to be hauled up short, to be criticized and corrected. When people were euphoric, the prophets spoke of doom. When their listeners despaired, the prophets offered hope. Always they seemed to go contrary to the prevailing mood, and that is why their lives were so distraught. The true prophets tell us things we are ill-prepared to hear, things we may not want to hear. They do not confirm our own beliefs or ratify what we would have done without them. They challenged their first hearers, and they challenge us. If we find ourselves feeling comfortable with the prophets, with Amos and Isaiah and Micah, we probably have not heard what they are saying to us.

The Relevance of the Prophets

If we take seriously this warning against presuming to understand or to accept the prophets too quickly, we are ready to see what message they have for our time. Though they were sometimes transported out of themselves by a kind of Hamlet's madness, they did not utter a garbled and meaningless word. The Greek oracles spoke ambiguously, in terms that could be interpreted several ways. Croesus was told, for example, that if he went to war a great kingdom would fall. What he did not realize was that the oracle meant his own kingdom! But by and large those who first heard the Hebrew prophets knew quite well what was being said. They predicted the fall of Samaria and of Jerusalem. Then

49

they said that Jerusalem would be restored. The message was clear, and much of it came to pass. The prophets were not dreamers, living in another world, out of contact with reality. They were more aware of the course of events than their more prosaic and levelheaded opponents. The prophets called a spade a spade; sin, sin; and a dangerous public policy, the folly that it was.

We would like sometimes to deny that these old prophets have anything to say to us, but we cannot. At times it is comforting to find in the margins of our Bibles "Hebrew obscure." It may, after all, mean something else. But the Hebrew may be plain as daylight, and no commentator can give us any comfort in uncertainty. The prophets clearly swept aside religion which concentrates exclusively on peace of mind. They rejected a faith which speaks only of what God does for us and says nothing of what we must do for him. The prophets looked frankly and without pretense at the weakness and waywardness of the human heart. They did not deny or cover up the real hardship that even God's people will have to bear. They tell us that it is possible to be patriotic in unfortunate ways, to develop a self-justifying blindness to the faults of our own people. They tell us that our most vicious enemies may be instruments used by God against a people who serve him only in name. They remind us that religion has something important to say about what we have, and about how we got it, and about what we will do with it. The prophets speak to us about him in whom alone we find life, and they tell us eloquently of his readiness to save from despair those who will turn to him. And perhaps most important of all, they show us what a true prophet is like, so that we may recognize those in our own time who are speaking the truth, the sometimes hard and always unbelievable truth, that God would have us hear and obey.

Chapter 4

The Outskirts of His Ways:
The Book of Job

> Lo, these are but the outskirts of his ways;
> and how small a whisper do we hear of him!
> But the thunder of his power who can understand?
> —Job 26:14

Carl Sandburg objected to the expression "more truth than poetry" because he contended that poetry often expresses truth which cannot be stated in any other way. What we call fiction often also lays bare the facts of human existence as nothing else can do it. The imaginative writer is not hampered by little details. He or she can heighten and dramatize the important while neglecting the insignificant. By means of a story, a writer can probe the hidden recesses of the human heart, exposing thoughts and motives that remain hidden to those who are only interested in visible data.

We are aware that what the fiction writer describes did not really happen. But we know that it could have happened and that something like this is taking place all the time. We could have easily overlooked these important events if the writer had not called them to our attention. Like an artist, he or she has drawn a bit of human experience as seen through his or her own eyes. Now the everyday incidents of which we were dimly conscious are connected in a meaningful pattern.

51

Jesus was just such an artist with words. He told more than thirty stories about farmers, servants, kings, housewives, and travelers. Circumstances and characters were drawn from everyday experience to create fictional accounts of great interest. The parable of the prodigal son tells us about God's forgiving nature and about man's need to be forgiven. It presents truth without which we would indeed be poor and ignorant.

When Richard Wright published his first short story, he was taken to task by his pious grandmother, who could not distinguish it from a lie. How impoverished we would be if we eliminated all imaginary accounts from our libraries! How much religious literature would have to go—*Pilgrim's Progress, Paradise Lost, The Robe,* and a substantial part of the Bible itself! If we insisted on the historical facts only, we would have to dispense with that profound and helpful study of man and God, the Book of Job.

Who was Job? In one sense, he is really the unknown author of the book by that title. Job as we know him was the creation of a writer who lived a few centuries before Christ. In telling of Job's woes and his struggle to find meaning in life, the author is disclosing his own inner conflicts. He shows us his own doubts, which the religion of his own day was unable to answer. He reveals to us his wrestlings with the riddle of life. He tells us something of the faith which emerged from these wrestlings. Cries which the author hardly dared to express are placed on the lips of Job. Alternating moods of trust and uncertainty, of loyalty to God and rebellion against him, reflect the struggle which took place in the writer's own soul.

In another sense, Job is every person. He represents you, the reader, as you seek to make sense of the world around you. If you have never thought in the way Job does, you could do so after reading his words. You can grasp his meaning because something like this has been your experience also. Or it could easily be your own experience if you were involved in some tragedy. You are eager to know the outcome of Job's struggle because you can identify his cause with your own.

The Prologue of Job, Chapters 1—2

Job is described as a man of fabulous prosperity. He possessed cattle and servants without number. He had more sons than daughters, a favorable ratio by Old Testament standards. And he was a devout person, offering sacrifices to atone for his children's errors when he did not even know of any. He was generous toward men and reverent toward God.

In the Book of Job, the Satan is one of God's messengers who has the task of seeking out and accusing wrongdoers. He is a kind of detective and prosecuting attorney in one. He goes here and there on the earth to spy on the activities of persons and to report back to God. God is sure that he has found nothing reprehensible in Job, but the cynical Satan is not convinced. Does Job worship God for nothing? Is he not well rewarded for his faithfulness? Doesn't Job know on which side his bread is buttered? What if he were less fortunate? What if he had nothing? What would happen to his religion then?

Job is put to the test to discover whether or not his devotion to God is genuine. Four messengers come quickly, one on the heels of another, with dire news. The cattle and servants are destroyed. Alas, the children have perished as well. Job is shaken. Instead of blaming God, however, he blesses his Creator and resigns himself to the loss.

The scene shifts back to heaven, where all of these earthly events are controlled. Perhaps, the Satan suggests, Job's love for his family was not as great as he had pretended it was. He can well bear their loss and still go on. A man will give up anything if his own life is spared.

But if his own body is attacked, he will lose his reserve and show his true colors. So a more serious test is carried out. Job is stricken with a horrible skin disease. He now sits on the city dump, to which he has been banished because of his disgusting, contagious condition. He scrapes his itching body with bits of broken pottery.

No doubt the writer had in mind elephantiasis, so called because of the horrible swelling and deformation which are its symptoms. Job is so disfigured that his friends do not recognize him. Elephantiasis is fatal, but it may run its course for several painful years before death comes. Large swellings appear on the body. These fester and then crust over. The skin blackens, splits, and falls off. There is much loss of weight and lack of sleep. The eyes water. Breathing is labored. Delusions and nightmares occur. The mouth emits a foul odor. Pain, fever, and itching become unbearable. Most distressing of all, in the time of Job, no pity could be expected from one's fellows. The ill person was regarded as the object of God's punishment. Along with other criminals, he was regarded with contempt.

In spite of his terrible affliction, Job refuses to curse God as his wife suggests. "Shall we receive good at the hand of God," he asked, "and shall we not receive evil?" We do not obey God and submit to him only as long as he is kind to us. We take him for better or for worse. We commit ourselves completely to him. This is the attitude Job expresses in chapter 2, but we shall see quite a different attitude in what follows!

Like a flock of vultures, Job's three friends come to "comfort" him. But they have not come merely to reassure and to help. Like many well-meaning visitors, they only increase the sick man's misery. Seeing their friend transformed from a community leader to a miserable wretch, they remain in stunned silence for several days. There follow many chapters of completely different material, the dialogues of Job and his friends.

There are sharp differences between chapters 1—2 and the materials which follow. The so-called Prologue is a narrative style, and what follows is in the regularly accented lines of Hebrew poetry. The Prologue is a succinct and rapidly-sketched account of a great man reduced to misery. What follows is a tedious, drawn-out story in which nothing really happens. The Prologue deals with events in heaven, and what follows takes place among human beings on earth. Job and his three friends know nothing about the test proposed by Satan. If they had known about the test, they would have had no difficulty explaining what happened to Job. As it is, they seek endlessly for some explanation. And Job shows none of the patience he had demonstrated in the Prologue.

Several explanations have been given for the differences between the Prologue and the poetic portions of Job. The most plausible one is that the writer made use of a much older story about Job which he incorporated into his book without substantial change. In much the same way, Shakespeare made use of the old story of Hamlet and enriched it with his superb poetry.

Job and His Friends

What do you say to someone who expresses discouragement and hopelessness? One helpful way to respond is to say, "Let's talk about it. When did you begin to feel this way?" By your words and attitude, you show that it is all right to feel discouraged. The friend tells how he or she feels, talks it through, and begins to feel better.

But often we do not answer a discouraged person in this way. We say, "Come on, buck up! Stop feeling sorry for yourself." Or we tell the unhappy person about someone else whose situation is a lot worse. Or we suggest that the person pray about it and assure him that this will make him feel better (implying that if he had been praying all along, he wouldn't have fallen into this mood). These are ways of saying, "You shouldn't feel discouraged. It's your own fault. You can easily change your mood if you want to do so." Now your friend not only feels discouraged but guilty as well!

This is the kind of unhelpful encounter that occurs between Job and his three friends. Job expresses the depths of his agony in chapter 3. He curses the day of his birth, as though it were a living thing which he could blame for his troubles. His life has become so meaningless that Job wishes it had never begun. Job is not patient in the poetic portions of the book, but he is refreshingly honest. He lets it all hang out. I recall a young minister whose daughter had been killed in an accident. As he stood by the casket, a parishioner asked, "Doesn't she look nice?" The minister looked at the lifeless body and replied, "Hell no, she's dead!"

The three friends of Job are surprised and angered by his expression of grief. They try to minimize his feelings and persuade him to change them. They pour scorn on him, and when he persists in asserting his dismay, they condemn him.

Eliphaz, Bildad, and Zophar repeat over and over the dogma of retribution: God punishes the wicked and rewards the righteous. This idea is found in many parts of the Bible, notably the Psalms, Proverbs, and Deuteronomy. The writer of Psalm 37 declares his experience:

> I have been young, and now am old;
> yet I have not seen the righteous forsaken
> or his children begging bread. (Psalm 37:25)

This is a lovely thought, and it may be an incentive to live a clean, upright life. The only trouble with this teaching is that it simply does not fit the facts! Evil people get away with their cruelties for a long time, and many of them seem to have all they want. And good people often suffer far more than they deserve.

This was true of Job. Not only had he lost his wealth and his family, but he had suffered unspeakable pain in his own body. In chapters 29—30, the writer skillfully describes Job's loss of status in the community. He was once a respected leader:

> Men listened to me, and waited,
> and kept silence for my counsel. (Job 29:21)

Persons in need had come to Job for help, and he had played the role of Lord Bountiful. But now that he had nothing, he was a byword and an object of scorn. Everyone shared the view of Job's three friends that Job was being punished for some hidden sin. They wanted no contact with this evil man.

But the point of the story is that Job had done nothing wrong. In fact, he had done many right things. In the "cleansing oath" of chapter 31, Job calls down wrath on his own head if he is guilty of any of a long list of evils: dishonesty, adultery, cruelty, greed, idolatry, and lack of hospitality. The standards Job here applied to himself would make most of us uneasy if we used them to measure ourselves. Few other persons in the Bible came up to these high requirements. Though a person of great wealth and status, Job saw his slaves as persons to be treated with respect:

> Did not he who made me in the womb make him?
> And did not one fashion us in the womb? (31:15)

Here is a concept of equality and of respect for persons which we are still trying to grasp twenty-five centuries after Job!

In spite of all his generosity and concern for others, Job suffered unlimited pain. This was even more baffling for Job and for persons living in the Old Testament era than it would be for us, for little was said in that time about life after death. There are few certain references to life after death in the Old Testament, and these suggest a kind of dim, meaningless existence. This meant that any rewards for good behavior had to come in this life or not at all. That is why Job cried out in agony to God:

> Let me alone, that I may find a little comfort
> before I go whence I shall not return,
> to the land of gloom and deep darkness. (10:20-21)

Job's Encounter with God

Job did not abandon God and curse him. On the other hand, he did not accept his fate without murmur. He spoke words similar to those of the psalmist, "My God, my God, why hast thou forsaken me?" (Psalm 22:1). He wrestled with doubts and fears. He alternated between quiet trust and restless rebellion. He accused God of playing with him as a cat teases a mouse. At other times he felt altogether abandoned by his Creator. He could not understand what he had done to deserve this fate. He never doubted that God exists. He assumed that God is in control of human affairs. But Job often wondered if God is an enemy or a friend. He asked disturbing questions. He made some shocking statements about God and about his relationship to mankind.

Here the deepest issue of the Book of Job comes to the fore. What is the relation between God and mankind? Does God simply take care of those who obey him, as the three friends insist? Or is there undeserved suffering in the world? If there is undeserved suffering, what does the sufferer have a right to expect from

God? What hope does he have? Should God be obeyed in expectation, or should he be defied in anger? These are shocking questions. They call in question the very foundations of religion. As the three friends put it, Job's attitude is a hindrance to meditation before God (15:4).

Job's suffering, real as it was, was not his heaviest burden. The pain pointed beyond itself to something far more frightening. Job felt he had been abandoned by his Lord. If he could be assured that God was still with him, if he could be shown that his service was not wasted, if he could be vindicated by God's stepping in to say that Job had acted and spoken rightly, the man of Uz would willingly suffer any torment. He would gladly step through the gates of death, if there he could feel the touch of a reassuring hand. In answer to the Satan's challenge, we may say that Job does serve God for his own sake and not simply for the material benefits he has received. When these benefits are taken away, however, Job wonders if God himself has also departed.

The answer Job received from God, according to chapters 38—41, was not an answer at all. It was not a statement that could be set down in a sentence or in a sermon. It was not a verdict of guilty or not guilty. It was the living, uplifting presence of God himself. Again and again God appeared to the people of the Bible—to Moses, to Amos, to Isaiah. He disclosed himself fully in Jesus Christ. Indeed, it is only because he chooses to step out of the shadows that we know anything about him at all. Otherwise, all our talk and all our thoughts about him are nothing more than confused speculations like those expressed by Job and his friends.

The first thing that God said, when he suddenly appeared out of the whirlwind of uncontrollable power, was a question addressed to Job: Who is this who darkens counsel with ignorant words? Who is this person who dares to discuss matters about which he can know nothing? Suddenly we find ourselves being questioned, challenged. It is not God who must answer us; it is we who must answer him. God emerges like a lighthouse out of a fog. The lighthouse does not have to move, and we cannot complain that it is in the wrong place. If we would come safely into harbor, we must accept the position of the lighthouse and correct our course in relation to it. We may not question the wisdom of what God has done or challenge his behavior. We need to correct our own thoughts and our own behavior to conform to his perfect wisdom.

One thing Job saw when he finally confronted God must become clear to us as well. He realized how silly he had been in demanding that God confirm his righteous acts. He had been trying to find God, not in order to serve him but in order to use him for Job's own purposes. He had not been guilty of any single sin, but he had separated himself from God in his satisfaction with his own commendable behavior. He would have to cast this pride aside in order to approach God. As Artur Weiser put it in *Das Buch Hiob:*

> Man must first lose this last hold before he stands in the great aloneness over against God, where the vision, no longer blurred by its own will, rises into the mystery of God, in which it feels the pulse beat of God's heart.[1]

Job felt God's heartbeat whenever he was able to put himself and his own demands to one side. Rather, having found God he no longer needed to seek his own purposes.

Beginning in the thirty-eighth chapter of Job, we catch a vision of the world and its Maker which rivals the picture in the first chapter of Genesis. We are led away from the troubled days and nights of a suffering soul. A sick person has a distorted and unbalanced idea of what life is all about. Usually the invalid sees nothing but his or her own little corner of the world and does not care for that. But there is much more to God's world than the little bit that any one of us can see. Let us look at God's great world as displayed in Job.

These chapters rehearse the wonders of the natural world; the heavenly bodies, the sea with its vast stretches, the changes of weather, and the powerful storms which come from nowhere. The writer is fascinated with the abundance of living things that God has made and put upon this earth. Many of these things are never seen by the eyes of men. "Full many a flower is born to blush unseen,/and waste its sweetness on the desert air."[2] God is the most wasteful of all workers. He has products to throw away, creations which no one will ever see except himself.

The world seems like one great zoo, in which God has placed the most peculiar animals for his amusement. The great ungainly hippopotamus, the tough-skinned crocodile—what a sense of humor God must have to make these strange creatures! The sea and sea monsters, so feared in ancient times, so magnified in the imagination of humans, are docile and domesticated subjects of God's power. The horse, coming into common use in warfare at the time Job was written, was, to the writer, a strange work of God. Always restless, starting at the sound of the battle trumpet, eager for conflict, unswerving in its headlong plunge into the midst of danger, majestic in its beauty—this also was the work of the master Designer. God seemed to be a great planner, a clever schemer, a never-satisfied deviser of new things to delight the eye. What impresses the observer is not so much the order and purpose of God's world but its overflowing abundance, its vastness beyond comprehension. God delights in his world. He finds it very good. When he laid its foundation, the morning stars sang for joy. There is much more to the world than the experiences of human beings. How could Job comprehend the world or understand its Maker on the basis of his shortsighted view?

How different this is from the first chapter of Genesis! There man stood at the very center of God's world. He was created last, as the climax of God's work. All things were made subservient to him. Even the sun and moon were conveniences for man, to help him keep track of time and dates. But here in Job, man is moved out of the center of creation. Many creatures are described which persons have never seen. Others have ways which human beings cannot comprehend. All of the vastness of the sky and sea and land is subservient to God, but it eludes the grasp of men like Job. There is much of God's world and of God himself which lies beyond our limited vision. We are not the only creatures for which he is concerned. When we become preoccupied with our own troubles and interests, we fail to see the universe beside which our little area of concern and short span of life are reduced to nothing.

Those who first read these dialogues were shocked by the way in which Job questioned God and by the fact that his three friends could not refute him. Someone added the speeches of Elihu (chapters 32—37) in order to do this, but they add nothing to the hackneyed assertions of Eliphaz, Bildad, and Zophar.

In the Epilogue (42:7-17), we return to the old folk story of Job. Here God condemns the three friends and rewards Job by restoring his family and former wealth. The writer of the Dialogues (3—27; 29—31; 38—42:6) has taken this old story, with its familiar happy ending, and has inserted into the narrative a penetrating and exhaustive study of man and God. The questions Job raises in these Dialogues cannot be answered simply by restoring his lost status.

A Christian Response to Questions Raised by Job

What can a Christian in the twentieth century say about the questions raised by Job? I do not want to seem as cruel and insensitive as his friends were. In fact, I see no reason to doubt the validity of Job's feelings or those of anyone else who suffers. I do not think we can tell such persons how they ought to feel.

59

But we can place our own experiences alongside theirs. We can bear witness to what we ourselves have seen and heard.

1. Job asked, *Why do I suffer?* There are many causes of human misery. Some of it we bring on ourselves by the foolish choices we make. Some ill health, for example, may be due to poor eating habits. Much human suffering is due to accidental circumstances which no one can foresee or prevent. Some hardship, whether God causes it or only permits it, may be punishment for wrongdoing.

But good people sometimes suffer—precisely because they are good! The prophets chose to proclaim God's word and were imprisoned and put to death for it. Jesus warned his disciples that following him would bring hardship and even martyrdom. Even more important than Job's question about the origin of suffering is the decision about how we will respond to it. There are ways of transforming unfortunate circumstances into opportunities for growth and service.

2. Job asked, *What is God really like?* One idea we can dismiss immediately is the God depicted in the Prologue and Epilogue to the Book of Job. God does not have to subject persons to tests like this in order to find out whether or not they are sincere. God does not play games with people, giving, taking away, and then giving again. He does not watch callously while one of his children is mistreated.

The majestic, mysterious God of Job 38—42:6 is in harmony with the picture we see elsewhere in the Bible, but it is not the whole picture. It shows the power of God but not his loving concern for humankind. The Gospels tell us of God's sending his only Son to share our life and to reveal God's love for us. Jesus healed the sick and raised the dead, showing that God cares about persons who suffer as Job did. Jesus encouraged persons to seek God in prayer and to ask for his help. "O that I knew where I might find him!" Job cried out (23:3). It is not always easy to find God because of the doubts and uncertainties that interfere. Jesus came to help us remove these doubts and uncertainties.

3. A third question Job asked was, *How can I find vindication?* Job had lived a commendable life. As the writer has portrayed him, he is almost faultless. Job would like to hear some word of approval from God. In fact, he is more interested in receiving this than in getting back his family and his health. He wants to know that his efforts to be good were not meaningless or useless.

Job is right about the importance of doing what is good. A person who has a conscience and follows it is to be commended. Jesus called those who do the will of God his true brothers and

60

sisters. But if we are good and then demand that God recognize and reward our goodness, we show a spirit of pride which tends to nullify our best achievements. The model of truly good persons are those whom Jesus commended for feeding the hungry, clothing the naked, and visiting the sick. They did it without realizing they were doing anything worthy of praise (Matt. 25: 31-46). Unless goodness is coupled with humility, it becomes pride and self-righteousness.

For the Christian, the object of life is not to be so good that we receive at last God's commendation. We begin with an acknowledgement that we have done those things we ought not to have done and have failed to do those things which we ought to have done. Then we turn to God in faith and receive the assurance of his mercy. We then fulfill acts of service to mankind and of obedience to God, not in order to accumulate merit but in order to show gratitude for what God has already done for us. Thus the Christian life is calm obedience in the assurance of God's love, not a frantic effort to prove that we are OK.

About one matter Job was right. He said he would have to receive his reward in this life, before he died, or not at all. There is a healthy here-and-now atmosphere in Job. Christians believe in life after death, but not as an escape from the demands of this life. If we do not find God before we die, we can scarcely hope to know him after we die. Unless we begin now to live what the Gospel of John calls "eternal life," we cannot hope to discover it after death. Thus the Christian's hope is for endless fellowship with God, a hope which gives strength and meaning to our present sojourn with God. This hope does not rescue us from the ambiguous choices and hard realities of everyday life right now.

I find myself reading the Book of Job again and again, finding things in it which I had not noticed before. The questions raised in Job are still with us and are still not completely answered. The insights that come to me as I read this book take on new meaning for me as my personal experience deepens and changes with the passing years. I hope you will treasure this book and read it many times.[3]

A Guide for Reading the Book of Job

I suggest that you read the Book of Job a chapter or two at a time, making use of the brief notes given here.

Chapters 1—2. The Satan was conceived as a heavenly being whose function was to watch persons and report their behavior— a kind of CIA agent. He agreed that Job appeared to be a good man, but he cynically suggested that Job would lose his religion quickly if his possessions and his health were removed. How stable is your own faith in God? Under what circumstances would you renounce it? Notice that Job is described as very patient here (1:20-22 and 2:9-10), but in what follows he is anything but patient.

Chapter 3. Job curses the day of his birth. Have you ever been so discouraged that you wanted to die? Have you ever wondered why you were ever born? Is such a feeling ever justified?

Chapters 4—5. Eliphaz glibly tells Job to trust in God. Here the familiar dogma is asserted that evil people are punished and good people are rewarded. This will be repeated a dozen times in the Book of Job. Eliphaz also states that in the sight of God no one (including Job) can claim to be righteous. No one deserves to be rewarded. All Job can do is to ask for God's help, and God will surely answer him.

Chapters 6—7. Job complains of his suffering and rebukes these friends who will not try to understand it. He asks what he has done to deserve all this affliction. He turns from the friends and begins to pour out his complaint to God in a most eloquent expression of grief.

Chapter 8. Bildad asserts the righteousness of God. He will reward those who seek him. Instead of relying on his own brief experience, Job should rely on the old traditions that have been handed down. These show that God rewards the righteous and punishes the wicked. Bildad refuses to admit that Job may be an exception to this old rule.

Chapters 9—10. Job asks how he can even approach God. How can he prove that he is innocent? A sense of futility and meaninglessness settles over him. In chapter 10, Job lectures God about the strangeness of his ways.

Chapter 11. What Job has just said is shocking to Zophar. If Job was not guilty of sin before this, his questioning of God is certainly sinful! Zophar tells Job to straighten up.

Chapters 12—14. Job 12:2 is intended as irony. Job knows that God is all powerful; he does not need to be told. He also assumes that God knows everything and will therefore see through the pretenses in the speeches of his comforters. Why do they feel that they have to tell lies on God's behalf? Job turns to God and pleads his case, like a prisoner before a judge. Man's life is short, and God ought to show mercy toward him.

Chapter 15. Eliphaz opens the second round of speeches by calling Job a hindrance to meditation. In stinging words he belittles the suffering man. Wicked persons (including Job?) will be punished by God.

Chapters 16—17. Job rebukes Eliphaz and continues his complaint.

Chapter 18. Bildad is angry because Job will not accept the teaching of his friends. He continues to speak of the fate of the ungodly, meaning obstinate persons like Job.

Chapter 19. Job complains of the torment to which he is being subjected. The callous words of these "comforters" are the worst of the sufferings he has to bear. Verses 23-27 have been variously interpreted. Job hopes for a redeemer who will be able to plead his case before God successfully.

Chapter 20. Zophar continues to expound on the fate of the wicked.

Chapter 21. Job asks why many evil persons seem to prosper. The statement that they are always punished is simply untrue. In Job's own case, a good man does not receive the reward which the friends say will always come to such a person.

Chapter 22. By now the friends are convinced that Job must be guilty of terrible crimes against God. Only thus can they explain his suffering. Eliphaz appeals to Job to humbly seek God's help. If he will repent, God will hear him.

Chapter 23. Job would like to find God. Surely God would listen to his complaint. But God is nowhere to be found.

Chapters 24—27. There appears to be some displacement of materials in these chapters. The following are probably to be assigned to Zophar and Bildad instead of Job: 24:18-20, 22-25; 26:5-14; 27:8-23.

Chapter 28. This is an interesting poem about wisdom, but it does not belong in the Book of Job.

Chapters 29—31. Job speaks of his former status as a person of importance. His humiliation has been as painful as any physical suffering. Chapter 30 is a final statement of Job's misery. Chapter 31 is a cleansing oath. Job calls down evil upon himself if he has been guilty of dishonesty, sexual abuses, mistreatment of poor persons, greed, or idolatry. Not many persons today could pass all of the tests which Job applied to himself here!

Chapters 32—37. The speeches of Elihu are an intrusion supplied by someone who felt that Job got off too easily. The young Elihu feels that he can succeed where the three older men failed. But he simply asserts the old dogma that suffering is punishment for sin. If Job will now turn to God, he will find healing. It's the old refrain of "Trust and Obey." Elihu asserts the majesty of God but fails to understand the misery of Job.

Chapters 38—41. At last, here is God's answer to Job. He tells Job that a mere mortal like Job has no right to challenge God. He cannot even understand the ways and purposes of God. He cannot accuse God of wrongdoing. In 40:3-5 and 42:1-6, Job accepts this judgment against himself.

Chapter 42:7-17. Here Job receives a completely different answer from the one in the previous chapters. Instead of being rebuked by God and told to accept his fate, he receives more than he had before his suffering began! As explained in the introductory pages, these verses are part of the old story which the author of Job used as a framework for his poetic discourses. Whereas the poetic part ends with a rebuke to Job, the old story ended happily with a reward for Job and a rebuke to his friends.

Chapter 5

Man Before God in the Psalms

Our Place in God's World, Psalm 8

A man looked at his watch and kissed his wife good-bye. To her he was a companion and lover. To the children who clutched his pant legs, he was a source of security. As he walked into the office, he greeted his secretary, to whom he represented authority. In the course of the day, he talked with salesmen who saw him as a customer. At lunch he associated with other workers who thought of him as a friend. Once he was called into the company president's office and treated as a subordinate. On the way home, his car was involved in a wreck. Persons passing by had pity on him because they saw him as an anonymous victim. An ambulance took him to a hospital, where he was treated as a patient. If the man had died, he would have been handled like a corpse.

Which of these ways of viewing the man is the correct one, if any? In each case the man's identity is determined by his relationship to someone else. Psalm 8 sets forth human nature and identity in relationship to God. We can know who we are if we know who God is. Let us see what the Psalm says about God and about human beings.

Psalm 8 speaks of God as the One who remembers and visits man. A literal translation of vs. 4 reads: "What is man that you remember him, and the son of man that you visit him?" The Psalm does not offer a speculative statement that God is almighty, or eternal, or all-knowing. It begins with human experience of God, our awareness that he has remembered us and that he comes to see us. It is not what God is but what God does that grasps the attention of the psalmist. "Oh yes, there he is. And there is his wife. I wonder how the children are doing. They must be in high school by now." What God does is to remember people and to check on them. After eight years of absence, I went back to a barber shop in upper Manhattan that I had frequented before. The barber immediately recognized me and asked how my work was going. The psalmist here speaks of God as one who has the same kind of intimate concern for us.

God is the one who visits human beings. The central message of the whole Bible is that the barrier which separates man and God has been broken from his side. He has come to us. He comes to us. He will come to us. He will not leave us alone, even when we long for a little privacy from his searching glance (Psalm 39:13). The problem of the Bible is not how to find God but how we may live for one instant without his knowledge and his presence. He is the Supervisor who is always just a stride away. A man who sometimes works the night shift told me he liked it better because all the white-collar men are away and he can do his work the way he chooses to do it. The world we live in is not on a night shift. It is a God-visited world, one in which God knows what we are doing and holds us responsible for obeying his will.

But this is not all that the psalmist says about God. God dwells with mankind, but he is also exalted above the heavens. His glory is chanted by babes and infants. God has successfully restrained the forces of evil. He has established the moon and the stars. The Psalm begins and ends with the refrain:

> O Lord, our Lord
> how majestic is thy name in all the earth!

God is far more than the companion of man. The distant reaches of the universe look to him for a sign that they may continue as before. Not a star is born without his will; not an electron runs its speedy course without his plan. The knowledge of the person who wrote Psalm 8 was pitifully restricted. The sky seemed little more than a few miles away, and the stars seemed but poor imitations of the gleaming sun. Only a few thousand square miles of the earth's surface were known to him. Yet even this vastness of God's creation filled the psalmist with awe. He could not understand how the God who created all this could condescend to be his friend!

> When I look at thy heavens, the work of thy fingers,
>   the moon and the stars which thou hast established;
> what is man that thou art mindful of him,
>   and the son of man that thou dost care for him?

How does the psalmist know that God has made all these things? How does he know that God remembers human beings? How does he even know that there is a God? He does not tell us. The Psalm is not a logical argument to convince us that these things are true. The writer is simply stating what he believes and what he has found to be true during many years of study and worship. He bears testimony to the long tradition of the Israelites, compresses centuries of experience as it has been examined and refined within the community of faith. What amazes the psalmist is that this sacred tradition about God seems to contain two incompatible features: that God is majestic in power and also involved in the life of persons. God is the one who rules the universe and also the one who has time to visit man.

This paradox of God's nature is left unresolved, and the psalmist examines the place of man in the presence of God. Once I visited a bakery and was introduced to the cake-icer. The cake-icer is not a baker, but he has an important role to play. All of us are like him. We have a place in God's plan, a place to fill, a task to do. "Thou hast made him a little lower than God," said the psalmist. Man is more than an animal, and among the creatures of earth he rules like a god. But man must look above himself to the One who gives significance and purpose to his life. Without the baker, the cake-icer can do nothing. Without God, our place is lost, our importance is nothing. We may be customers, or friends, or corpses. But we are not really human beings. Who are we? We are those who have been remembered and visited by the Lord of creation. We are not angels, and we are not supermen. The psalmist looks at the absurdity of our position and asks skeptically, "What is man?" as though the answer were: Nothing at all. Yet in the presence of God and by his decree we are something! Do we shrivel up and disappear in the awful presence of the Almighty? No, because God commands us to stand erect. He wants to pay us a visit. He wants to remind us of old promises and to refresh his acquaintance with us. God has business with his cake-icers!

We ought to carry ourselves with a kind of sober dignity because of what we learn in Psalm 8. We need not put on airs or blow ourselves up like a balloon, a hundred times bigger than we really are. But we can carry with us the thought of how majestic God is and how much he cares for us. He is Everything; we without him are nothing. Yet he sees us as those to whom he gives his attention, his care, and his love!

The Starry Heavens and the Moral Law, Psalm 19

Psalm 19 expresses two different moods. The first six verses tell us about the heavens and their grandeur. The last eight verses are about God and his laws intended to guide our lives. So different are these two sections of the Psalm that many scholars have said they were originally two separate poems that came together by accident. But I believe the two stanzas belong together in the same Psalm. It is the same God whom we see in the distant star and in the inner light of conscience. Immanuel Kant wrote, "Two things fill the mind with ever new and increasing wonder and awe—the starry heavens above me and the moral law within me."[1]

Of course, we could experience fear instead of awe when we look at the night sky. How vast is this world we live in! The nearest star, other than our sun, requires four years to cast its light upon us, so distant is it. The other stars are incalculable distances away, so far that the mind can scarcely grasp what the figures mean. We could well feel like sailors clinging to a raft on the surface of some limitless ocean. The starry heavens, with their limitless, impersonal depths could fill us with terror. There is no place here to cast an anchor, no safe harbor for man.

We could experience despair instead of awe when we look into the heavens. How the whole procession seems to go forward without waiting for us! The stars move according to timetables so regular that we can set our watches by them. The ancients called the planets "wanderers," but they do not wander at all. We now know that they follow predictable courses. Nothing we can do will change the movement of the stars or the sun. We feel helpless in their presence. Round and round, and on and on, the parade goes. The thought makes us wonder whether our lives are not also fated, chained to a great wheel, so that we are born and grow up and decline and die like the rising and setting sun, without ourselves having any say in the matter. The starry heavens with their message of changeless regularity could well fill us with helplessness and despair.

Looking at the night sky did not fill the psalmist with fear or despair. It filled him with awe, a feeling of solemn wonder. How great must be the God who made all these things and keeps them going, he thought. It was the presence of God in the world he has

68

created which kept it from being a fearful spectacle to the psalmist. How did he know that God is at work in the starry sky? He recognized the handwriting of an old friend. Every few weeks I get a letter from a friend. I recognize the handwriting and quickly open it because I know it will be an interesting and cheery note. The world that may seem strange and even forbidding to some people provoked awe and joy in the psalmist because he recognized there the handwriting of One he had met before, the God he knew quite well from a different kind of experience in another place.

The psalmist belonged to a special people who treasured a unique tradition. They remembered how God had intervened in the lives of their ancestors, calling them out of slavery in Egypt and giving them a new land. The tradition told of God's promises to their ancestors, promises which were to be fulfilled in their own lives. It told of God's steadfast and unchanging love for them. This magnificent memory regarding the past and this reassuring hope about the future was what held the people of Israel together. The psalmist looked up at the night sky from his rooftop in Jerusalem and then let his eyes drift downward to the surrounding houses. Inside the houses were his fellow Israelites, persons who nurtured and preserved the holy tradition about God's reaching out to this people and offering them his gifts. The psalmist could see the dim outlines of the Temple in the distance, a reminder of God's presence among his people. The psalmist had already met God and knew that he was loving and kind as well as all-powerful. So he could look up into the sky without fear or despair.

The heavens are telling the glory and the handiwork of God. One day speaks to another about it, with unceasing eloquence. Night declares unto night the wisdom of the One who made the stars. There is no speech. Quiet calms the air. Yet he who has ears and eyes will hear and see. The clear and shining truth will come to him. The words, the meaning, the purposes of God are clear. They echo through the chambers of the night. They are whispered on the wind. They are signaled by a blinking star. They are confirmed by the steady glow of a familiar planet.

Two things filled the philosopher Kant with awe—the starry heavens and the moral law. The psalmist turned from contemplating the heavens and thought about his own personal life. There he saw patterns as inflexible as the ones which guide the stars. There also he saw the handiwork of God. There are actions which we cannot enter into without destroying ourselves, just as the stars cannot depart from the courses in which God has set them.

But what are these forbidden actions? What is the moral law?

69

Human beings cannot agree on an answer. Many rules have a wide appeal, but none is universal. "Thou shalt not kill" would seem to be a fundamental rule, but there are many who ignore it. Even civilized nations recognize times when it is right to kill—in wartime, in self-defense, in punishment for crime. Many persons question the right to take life under any circumstances, but their views have not prevailed. How, then, can we speak of a moral law? If there is such a law, there is little agreement about what it says.

The psalmist derived his understanding of God's law from his people's experience with God over many centuries. Yahweh, the LORD, had entered into their history and had offered them freedom. When he met them at Sinai, he told them what he wanted them to do. They were to obey these commandments because he told them to do so and because of what God had done for them. Obeying the Ten Commandments was necessary to uphold the covenant between God and his people. Disobedience meant danger to the whole people. It meant forsaking their God and his ways. "You shall be holy, for I am holy," he told them. Immanuel Kant attempted to explain the moral law in a way that any reasonable person could accept, but the writer of Psalm 19 proclaimed a law which could only be understood by persons who had met Yahweh and had been called to participate in his covenant.

Most of us do not get overjoyed about laws. We recognize the need for them, but they seem to be a necessary evil. They keep us from doing some of the things we like to do. They interfere with our freedom. We are not pleased to learn that God has given us some rules to obey. Why should he meddle in our personal lives? What right has he to tell us that we must be respectful of other persons in our intimate sexual encounters? Why must we restrain our anger and our urge to hurt other persons? Why must we be honest with each other, when it is so comfortable to hide behind a front? The law of God does not seem like something to be glad about. It seems like something to be borne with resignation, if at all.

But the psalmist had a different view. He was glad that God had disclosed his will. The psalmist gladly accepted the way which was set before him because he knew that it led to life and to happiness. He was led to obey, not from fear of the consequences, but from sheer joy. The freedom and peace that comes only to those who heed God's command settled over his life. Not reluctantly but willingly he traced God's message and conformed to its requirements. Sometimes direction about how to live comes to us as a blessing and not as a curse. When educational leaders began stressing self-direction a few years ago, a cartoon appeared showing a distressed student asking a teacher, "Do we have to do what we want to do again today?" The psalmist would have understood that cartoon. He rejoiced in God's law. For him it was not a burden at all:

> the ordinances of the LORD are true
> and righteous altogether,
> More to be desired are they than gold,
> even much fine gold;
> sweeter also than honey
> and drippings of the honeycomb. (8-10)

In the hushed silence of God's presence, the psalmist looked inward upon his own heart. He was set within a vast and awe-inspiring universe, recognized as such even without the knowledge which science has made available to us. Moreover, the psalmist was aware of God's controlling hand in his own life, just as important and just as inescapable as God's rule of the natural world. Yet he himself had to decide whether or not he would accept and obey God's commandments. Perfect as God's law is, our obedience is not perfect. We are free to reject or to accept it. The psalmist reflected on the things he had done and had left undone. He asked for God's help:

> . . . who can discern his errors?
> clear thou me from hidden faults.
> Keep back thy servant from presumptuous sins;
> let them not have dominion over me! (12-13)

Starry heavens and moral law—they lead us to rejoice in the glory and wisdom of God. They also make us concerned about ourselves, that in our inner thoughts and our outward actions we might fulfill the destiny which the gracious God has planned for us. And so we may pray with the writer of Psalm 19:

> Let the words of my mouth and the meditation of my heart
> be acceptable in thy sight,
> O LORD, my rock and my redeemer.

How to Handle Guilt, Psalm 51

A horrible murder has been committed, and the police have no leads to the killer; but twenty people have given themselves up and confessed the crime. A certain woman is always spying on her neighbors and talking about their scandalous behavior; she sees suspicious signs of wrongdoing where others see nothing unusual. A man is tormented by sleeplessness and nightmares; during his waking hours he is constantly afraid of making mistakes. Another man asks for overtime and volunteers for the hardest jobs; he never seems satisfied unless he is driving himself. A woman takes a bath several times a day and still feels unclean. All of these persons may be preoccupied with guilt. You and I may not be like them, but we also have to come to terms with guilt. We have to discover the best way to deal with it.

The first suggestion that comes to our minds is that we should simply ignore it, pretend that it isn't there. We decide that it is a fairy tale handed down from the past but not to be taken seriously today. It is a remnant from childhood, when we were told that we would be punished for being bad. There are some who tell us that healthy and intelligent people need not feel guilt, no matter what they have done or failed to do. Yet there are others who warn us that guilt cannot be ignored. We must find out why we feel guilty. We must correct whatever it is that is causing the guilt. We must acknowledge real wrongdoing and do something about it. We must discover imaginary and unwarranted guilt feelings so that they may lose their power over us. Unless we come to grips with guilt, these counselors say, it could cripple or kill us.

If we cannot ignore guilt, we also cannot allow it to dominate our lives. We must not imagine, as many people do, that we have done wrong when we have not. We should not look for things for which to be sorry. We need not brood over every act and every thought, fearful that we may have broken some unwritten law. If it is useless to ignore guilt and foolish to allow it to dominate our lives, what can we do with it? How can we handle guilt healthily? How can we master our guilt instead of allowing it to master us?

This is the question that lies back of the Fifty-first Psalm. This penetrating prayer was written by someone who understood guilt. Note the first two verses, which seem to form a prologue to the whole Psalm:

> Have mercy on me, O God,
>   according to thy steadfast love;
> according to thy abundant mercy
>   blot out my transgressions.
> Wash me thoroughly from my iniquity,
>   and cleanse me from my sin!

Here the writer uses three different words for wrongdoing, which we translate "transgression," "iniquity," and "sin." He has something on his conscience that he wants to remove. He accepts his guilt and does not try to deny it.

But the psalmist in these same two verses uses three beautiful words for God's mercy. One of them means "favor." One of them means "steadfast love" or "covenant faithfulness." One of them means "compassion"—the kind of mercy Hosea said was missing from his troubled home. The writer assumes that he is a sinner, but he also knows that God is merciful. God does not look upon him in anger but in love. The same two verses tell of three things which God does for the sinner. He "blots out" the wrong. He "cleanses" and "washes" the sinner. Knowledge of God's loving concern for us enables us to make a clean breast of our mistakes. There is no need to cover them up or deny them.

The next few verses are a penetrating analysis of sin. "I know my transgressions, and my sin is ever before me." How good it is if we know our sin! If we have no conscience, no sense of what ought to be done, we destroy every possibility of living together with other persons. We may also endanger our own lives and our own happiness. Somehow we must find a sense of direction in order to survive, an awareness of when we have done wrong. A vague feeling of wrongness is not enough. We must know what it is we have done wrong, in order to confess it and to correct it.

A man came to me for counseling. He had been unfaithful to his wife, and this had begun to affect their relationship. She kept asking what was wrong with him, and he could not honestly say that nothing was wrong. He loved his wife and children and wanted to keep them. His wife came to the counseling session, and together we talked about what had happened. The husband explored some unhappy experiences of childhood and a resulting deep need for affection. He discovered that he had used his wife and other women to try to meet his own needs, seldom giving anything in return. He had been too easily hurt, too quickly discouraged, too disappointed in the intimacies of his own marriage. When he came to understand why he had deserted his wife, the need to do this became less pressing. He discovered genuine love for her, and she reciprocated with feelings that she had never shared with him before. Through self-understanding and confession he was able to find forgiveness and a new life.

"Against thee, thee only, have I sinned," said the psalmist. Here sin is seen as a personal offense against God. It is not the casual disregard of some rule written in a dusty book. It is a rejection of the God who has made us and who wills that we should find life in obedient service to him. When we do something that injures our bodies, or when we bring harm to other persons, we are abusing something precious which God has made. All sin is offense against God, and so it is to him that we must turn for pardon and renewal.

"I was brought forth in iniquity, and in sin did my mother conceive me," the psalmist writes. This does not mean that sexual intercourse is sinful. The Bible regards this act as a part of God's creation, which God beheld and declared to be good. Rather, the statement means that sin is radical. It belongs to his very existence as a human being. From the time he or she is born, a human being is no stranger to sin. Infancy is a time when one believes that he is omnipotent, that he is God. When the growing person continues to organize the universe about himself, refusing to acknowledge the rights of other persons and the claims of God, he is guilty of what we call the sin of pride. It is because the roots of this sin are so deep that we must deal with it seriously. We cannot drop a few old habits and take leave of an old acquaintance and suppose that we have dealt adequately with sin. Sin is radical, and it requires a radical remedy. Somehow we must be renewed to the very bottom of our souls. Otherwise, we will simply be treating the symptoms; the disease will soon break out again. That is why we must turn to God. Only he can renew us. We are too ill, too twisted, to help ourselves.

What is it that the sinner needs? He needs "truth in the inward being" (vs. 6). The essence of sin is the lie—the lie that one can get away with wrongdoing, that crime pays, that good is evil and evil is good. The beginning of sin is the rationalization, the process by which we convince ourselves that things are different from what they appear to be. There must be truth in the inward being, honesty in the sight of God. We must be willing to listen to what God tells us, open to the truth and not rigidly blind and defiant.

The sinner needs cleansing also. "Wash me, and I shall be whiter than snow" (vs. 7). Old deeds, old motives, and old thoughts must be purged away. The sinner must breathe the pure, clean air of freedom and joy. The broken bones of the crippled soul must be mended. The illness of sin must be replaced by health. The past must be forgotten because it has been forgiven. The sinner must have the cherished privilege of beginning again.

But honesty and cleansing are not enough. So pervasive and powerful is sin that when we are rid of it, our freedom is only temporary. We are not safe unless there is something more than freedom from sin. Our victory is only negative unless we are effectively armed against a recurrence. We must have power to deal with temptation, energy to cope with the threats that confront us. This is why the psalmist writes, "Create in me a clean heart, O God." He uses the special word *bara,* which is reserved for the original act of creation. It means making something from nothing, beginning all over again, not altering or patching but starting afresh. The sinner must be renewed by the power of God—not on the surface but in the depths of the self, not temporarily but for good. It is only when life is thus changed from within by God that we are able to overcome sin and to find the life which God offers us.

It was customary in the time of the psalmist to make a promise when asking a gift from God. The writer thinks over the things he could offer to God. He could bring a costly gift to the temple, a sacrificial animal to be offered on the altar. But he knows that God wants something more than this, something far more costly. God does not want our gifts; he wants us. He does not want blood or flesh; he wants a human being offered in love and service. And so the psalmist offers himself to God—"a broken and contrite heart." He has learned through self-appraisal and confession that he needs God and that God is merciful. And he has given himself to God.

Our Dependence on God, Psalm 90

Gratitude does not ooze from the Ninetieth Psalm. Some of the psalms become a bit tiresome in their constant reiteration of the steadfast love and mercy of God. Anyone who has lived five minutes in the real world is inclined to say, "Come off it!" to that sort of piety, especially if it is not balanced by a realistic look at the evil which sometimes obscures what God is doing for us.

The psalmist looks at life as it really is. He knows that we are not on our own. He knows that if the divine breath were taken away from this heap of dust which we are, we would become windblown dust once again. He knows that God is behind it all, but he isn't ringing any church bells in joy. He expresses his thanksgiving with a bit more reserve than many of the psalmists do because he has walked more closely with God than most persons do. And he has found that path to be a stony way.

The focal point of his disturbance is that third verse:

> Thou turnest man back to the dust,
> and sayest, "Turn back, O children of men!"

God is not simply calling on persons to repent in this verse. Instead, he is writing a final "No!" to the prideful ambitions of the creatures he has made. He is confusing the language of those who hope to build a tower to heaven and thus win fame. He is turning us back to the dust of our original state. Every sane person is aware of a law of averages that puts a vague upper limit on personal achievements and the length of life. Every good thing that we do comes up short at some kind of end. For the writer of Psalm 90, this end of all human endeavor was experienced as personal. He was not up against a stone wall, he was up against God. Always he was beating at doors that would not open. They could not be opened because Someone more than human had his foot pressed firmly against the threshold on the other side.

The baffling part of this experience is that we cannot escape the difficult by simply giving up. We cannot say, "OK, I cannot do what I want to do, and so I will do nothing at all." God sets a lower limit as well as an upper limit on what we do. Ahab paced the deck in quest of the whale, Moby Dick, and pondered his inescapable fate: "Here some one thrusts these cards into these old hands of mine; swears I must play these, and no others."[2] When we try to play other cards than the ones we have been dealt, a voice says, "Turn back, O man!" But if we throw our cards on the table and refuse to play any, there is an equally insistent voice at our ears.

But the psalmist sees more than these irksome restraints. When he comes to the end of his tether, God is there, not only to remind him that the tether has an end but also to provide something better than what the psalmist was seeking as he tried to break away. I have counseled with many persons who have begun by cursing God for refusing to let them have their own way. Many of them have ended by blessing God for providing an even better way. He is the bounds and limit, the disgusting "No" that echoes down at us from the corridors of glory which we long to enter, but he is also the final resort of those who would find what is truly good.

"Thou has been our dwelling place in all generations." It has been suggested that this line does not belong in the psalm because it reflects a different mood from the one just described. God does not turn men back and at the same time offer them a refuge, it is said. But the psalm is inconsistent because life is inconsistent. If we could see beyond the immediate experiences of the moment, we might see a reasonable pattern and an explanation of God's seemingly divergent actions. But we cannot see beyond the contradictions—not yet. There are times when we feel both deserted and undergirded, both the objects of God's anger and the recipients of his endless concern.

The permanence of God reverberates like a solid bass accompaniment through the flighty and uncertain melody of this psalm. The worshiper reaches back into her or his own memory, into the inherited traditions from the distant past, and even beyond this, into the days unknown when the everlasting hills were heaped up. No expanse of time can equal the continuing, plodding, patient changelessness of God. In our ambition, we come up against something hard and unyielding. We break ourselves against him, bitterly, and we finish by praising him gladly for the very inflexibility of his being and his purpose. A father whom we can wrap around our little finger is sometimes a convenience but rarely a support. The stolid permanence of the eternal God is something to reach for while we are getting our bearings, while we are trying to decide who we are and where we are going. We who live in such confused and uncertain times need to look longingly and gratefully to him for whom a thousand years is like a brief watch in the night.

Self-understanding is one of the gifts which God can give us. We need to be aware of his unchanging strength but also of our own brevity. "So teach us to number our days that we may get a heart of wisdom." The journalist Stewart Alsop has written with feeling about how his thinking changed when he realized that he had only about a year to live.[3] Yet all of us have a limited amount of time in which to discover the meaning of life, in which to give and receive love, in which to become what God calls us to be. We need not become frantic because of this knowledge, but we could be wiser and better persons than we sometimes are.

Steadfast love is another gift which Psalm 90 expects to receive from God. "Satisfy us in the morning with thy steadfast love, that we may rejoice and be glad all our days" (vs. 14). Some of the psalms are a bit plaintive about this matter of God's loyalty. They go back over the Exodus point by point, emphasizing the glorious things which God has done for his people in the past, and suggesting that he might get busy and do something like this for them once again. It was their unshakable conviction that this episode of glory in Israel's history was not a passing whim, some hobby that God took up for a time and then put aside for something else, but a permanent and indelible characteristic of his very nature. God's earnestness about his people, his clinging to them even when they have tried to cast him off, is what the psalmists mean by God's *chesed,* his "steadfast love." Psalm 90 cries out for it.

The prayer with which Psalm 90 closes brings us full circle from the impatience of frustration to the quiet of trust:

> . . . establish thou the work of our hands upon us,
> yea, the work of our hands establish thou it.

There is here the humble recognition that the work of our hands is an impermanent achievement. But there is also a yearning for the durability and strength which the blessing of God bestows upon the feeble efforts which we make in his name. The writer seems to say: "Here is what I've struggled to do, Lord, now you make something of it." For all those moments of helplessness— when a young person leaves home and you've had your last chance to influence him or her for good, when you've spent your last ounce of strength for some cause in which you believe and the outcome is still uncertain, when you sit down in agony trying to deny some awful message you've just been given on the telephone—here is a sincere prayer of a person who discovered the limits and explored them with his God: "Establish thou the work of our hands!" His belief that God was able to do this sustained him and lifted him up. It was the assurance that something permanently significant can be made from what is inherently temporary.

Psalm 90 is a prayer of thanksgiving, but it is not the horn-of-plenty, roasted-turkey, pumpkin-pie kind of Thanksgiving. It is a probing of the very ocean bottom of what it means to be, with all the glittering joys of life contrasted with the unbearable tragedies, the things we have received balanced against what we have been denied. Still, it is a thanksgiving prayer because it clings to the mercy of God while acknowledging the needs that make his mercy necessary. It is an avowal of our dependence which is really a holding on for dear life, a reaching out for the Hand to hold us which is sometimes felt to be thrusting us back. The psalm is about the restraining and sustaining God.

Some Thoughts About the Book of Psalms

The four psalms we have just discussed deal with the question of who God is and who we are. Who is God, not as a theological concept, but as a living person whose work intersects our own? Who are we, not considered by ourselves but in relation to the God who beckons us? These are questions which cannot be answered in a sentence or in a book. They must be explored in life, in prayer, in meditation upon the Scriptures, and in encounters with other persons. We cannot exhaust the many aspects of these questions in a lifetime. That is why the psalms approach these questions from so many angles and in so many different attitudes: joy, fear, hatred, exaltation, gratitude, anger, trust. The Psalms, like the Book of Job, frankly express many things that we have difficulty saying, especially in the presence of God. That is why the responsive readings in our hymnals are carefully expurgated of the more offensive parts of the psalms that are used. While we may not accept some things in the psalms, especially the bitter things that are said about the wicked, we can admire the honesty with which the writers speak of what they feel.[1]

I once classified the subject matter of all the verses in the first fifty psalms. The result was:

I. God	Percent
A. God in Nature	4.0
B. God in History	9.3
C. God's Law	0.6
D. Worship of God	5.3
E. God's Steadfast Love	4.9
F. God's Vindication of Righteous Persons and Punishment of the Wicked	26.4
G. God's Holiness and Righteousness	2.5
H. Pleas Addressed to God	19.0

II. Other Matters	
A. The Nature of Man	4.0
B. Description of the Good Man	2.6
C. Description of the Wicked	7.4
D. Sickness and Distress	4.1
E. A Sense of Sin—or Lack of It	4.2
F. Unclassified	5.7

The Psalms can provide a lifetime of joy and helpful guidance for meditation. Those who have a daily prayer time may wish to read through The Psalms every thirty days. Here is a scheme which makes it possible to do this without having too much to read on a single day:

Day	Psalms	Day	Psalms
1	1-5	16	76-80
2	6-10	17	81-85
3	11-15	18	86-90
4	16-20	19	91-95
5	21-25	20	96-100
6	26-30	21	101-105
7	31-35	22	106-110
8	36-40	23	111-118
9	41-45	24	119
10	46-50	25	120-125
11	51-55	26	126-130
12	56-60	27	131-135
13	61-65	28	136-140
14	66-70	29	141-145
15	71-75	30	146-150

Chapter 6

Judah's Hundred-Year Heart Attack

The Bible describes a "heart attack." It was unlike any other because it lasted more than a hundred years, and it involved the whole nation of Judah. But it was like a heart attack in other ways. For years before the attack itself, there were symptoms of the disease which were apparent to discerning observers. Most of the people of Judah, however, were not aware of what was happening beneath the apparent calm. Then the nation was subject to a massive thrombosis. For a time, it appeared that there would be no recovery. Politically, in fact, the nation was dead. But slowly it began to show signs of new life. The people had time to think about what had happened to them and about what they could do now. One thing was certain: They could never again be the same as they had been before. But they could be something else, something better.

Signs of the oncoming heart attack began to appear late in the seventh century B.C. Great changes took place among the nations surrounding Judah. Egypt became stronger. Babylon began to stir. The Empire of Assyria, which had dominated the area for more than a century, faltered and collapsed. Little nations like Judah enjoyed a new political and religious freedom. But optimism was premature, for a new power struggle was under way.

Whether they participated or not, the little nations were in danger of being hurt.

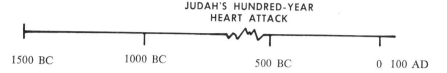

JUDAH'S HUNDRED-YEAR
HEART ATTACK

1500 BC   1000 BC   500 BC   0 100 AD

Jeremiah: The Prophet Set Apart

Professor James Muilenberg of Union Seminary used to describe this historical situation and then say, taking the role of God looking over the scene, "I believe I'll make Jeremiah." Jeremiah believed that God had made plans for him even before his birth. As a young man he heard the call of God. He tried to resist this call, to no avail. Again and again he protested that he did not want to speak what God told him to say. He was given a very difficult role, and he accepted it with great reluctance. He was told to "pluck up and to break down . . . to build and to plant" (1:10). His mission was to destroy an old and inadequate faith and to put a new one in its place.

"I have set you apart," God said to Jeremiah (1:5). This was true in many ways. He was set apart from his own family; they came to despise him and even threaten his life, possibly because he favored a reform which deprived them of their priesthood. He was set apart from family life; God willed that he should not marry or have children. He was set apart from the nation that he loved because he refused to endorse everything his nation did. He was set apart from kings and princes, whose policies he criticized. He was set apart from scribes, priests, and even the other prophets. He had few friends because few were willing to accept his message.

As he contemplated the evils which were about to come upon his people, Jeremiah trembled. He saw strange visions and heard terrible sounds. In my home town lived a man who sometimes stopped on a busy street, showed terror in his face, and then ran as fast as he could. People said it was because he could still hear the guns of Argonne and Verdun. Jeremiah heard the sounds of war also, but he heard them before they came:

> My anguish, my anguish! I writhe in pain!
>   Oh, the walls of my heart!
> My heart is beating wildly;
>   I cannot keep silent;
> for I hear the sound of the trumpet,
>   the alarm of war. (4:19)

81

For Jeremiah, being a prophet was not simply a matter of taking a message from God and delivering it to the people. This messenger read the letters that he carried, and they filled him with pain. The experience of bringing these awful tidings almost tore the prophet apart:

> My heart is broken within me,
> all my bones shake;
> I am like a drunken man,
> like a man overcome by wine. (23:9)

Those who heard Jeremiah preach must have thought of him as strong, forceful, and unflinching in his commitment to the truth. If they had known his private thoughts, however, they would have seen him in quite a different light. Jeremiah alone, among the prophets, has left us an intimate journal of his conversations with God.[1] Here he reveals his innermost self, and we see him as bitter, confused, and uncertain. Early in his ministry, he predicted the coming of a foe from the North. Jeremiah waited, but the foe did not come. He blamed God for this mistake, likening him to a stream in the desert that is now full, and now empty (15:18):

> O LORD, thou hast deceived me,
> and I was deceived. . .
> I have become a laughingstock all the day;
> every one mocks me. (20:7)

Jeremiah carried his complaints to God repeatedly, but he received little encouragement. Finally, God called on Jeremiah to do something he was always telling others to do: *return*. If Jeremiah would turn around, place himself in God's care, and guard his words more closely, God would make him strong and effective (15:19). Jeremiah recognized the truth of this advice at last:

> Heal me, O LORD, and I shall be healed;
> save me, and I shall be saved;
> for thou art my praise. (17:14)

Jeremiah got into trouble because of a sermon he gave at the gate of the Temple in Jerusalem. The city was a mountain fortress which had stood firmly against invaders for four centuries. In the previous century, it had held out while cities all around it fell to the enemy. It seemed to the people of Judah that God was protecting the city of Jerusalem and its Temple in a special way. They felt secure when they were in God's house. Imagine their surprise, then, when a prophet proclaimed that God himself would destroy the place. "I will make this house like Shiloh!" Jeremiah cried in God's name. (Shiloh was another temple which had been destroyed by the Philistines centuries earlier.)

Jeremiah said that the people had made the Temple a kind of hideout, like that which is used by a gang of robbers. After a series of crimes, they ran to it and said, panting, "We made it! We're safe!"

> Will you steal, murder, commit adultery, swear falsely,
> burn incense to Baal, and go after other gods that you have
> not known, and then come and stand before me in this house,
> which is called by my name, and say, "We are delivered!"—
> only to go on doing all these abominations? (7:9-10)

Those who heard Jeremiah were angry, not only because he criticized their actions but also because of the danger to which he exposed them. They believed that his words would have a tendency to bring about exactly what he predicted. Ancient people took the spoken word much more seriously than we do; for them, it was just as real as the object or event to which it referred. That is why some of them said that Jeremiah should die for what he had spoken (26:8-9).

Jeremiah was trying to say something which is still true: God holds us responsible for our actions. God expects something of us. He expects honesty, concern for our neighbors, loyalty to himself. If we neglect these things, we cannot find security and comfort in our religion. Going to church in order to praise God is a sham and a deception if we have not done our best to serve God every day. It may seem to be an obvious truth, but we forget it again and again.

Like the other prophets, Jeremiah watched and listened for some word from the Lord. Once he heard God speaking to him through an everyday occurrence. He happened to see a potter making a vessel by shaping it on a flat wheel that he turned with his feet. Something happened to spoil the work, and the potter simply gathered the damp clay together and started over. If a potter could begin again with his spoiled work, couldn't God do the same thing with his people? They had turned out so badly that Jeremiah sometimes wondered if there was any hope for them. But God seemed to be speaking to him through the potter, saying that there was still hope for the people if they would return to God and allow him to remake them (18:1-11).

But the people did not listen to Jeremiah until it was too late. Twelve years after he gave his sermon in the Temple, the Babylonians came to Jerusalem and took away its leaders. Ten years later, the Babylonians came a second time and carried on a long siege. This time they destroyed the Temple and took more captives. Cruel as they were, the Babylonians appeared to Jeremiah as the instruments of God's purpose. They were sent to punish the people of Judah for their disobedience. Jeremiah counseled his countrymen to surrender to these enemies, and for this he was branded a traitor.

During the long siege of Jerusalem, normal life and business stopped. We can imagine that the price of food climbed steeply, while the price of land fell. At that time, a relative of Jeremiah came to offer him a field for sale. The people of the Bible regarded their land as part of the family and tried to keep from selling it to strangers. But the war was so terrible and the future was so uncertain that one could hardly have blamed Jeremiah if he had refused to buy the field. But Jeremiah saw the event as another example of God's speaking to him, just as he had done when the potter spoiled his work. He paid seventeen silver shekels for the land and signed the deed before witnesses. He gave the deed to Baruch, his secretary, and told him to seal it in an earthenware jar in such a way that it would last a long time. "For thus says the LORD of hosts, the God of Israel: Houses and fields and vinyards shall again be bought in this land" (32:153. Buying the field was Jeremiah's way of betting on the future. It was a way of demonstrating his belief that the Babylonian invasion was not the final end of his country and its people.

Jeremiah felt that the old covenant or agreement which had held his people together and had bound them to God was no longer in force. It had been broken by the people of Judah when they disobeyed God. They could not expect God to fulfill his promises to Abraham and Moses because they had rejected his rule. But Jeremiah dreamed that God would offer them a new covenant. This would be a different agreement, not one that needed to be passed from one generation to another by the uncertain means of teaching the young. It would be internal, a matter of the heart, so instinctive that there would be no need to convince people to keep its requirements. Everybody would know and love God without having to be urged to do so (31:31-34).

Ezekiel Speaks of Freedom and Responsibility

Among the exiles who were taken to Babylon in the first deportation was Ezekiel, a prophet who was quite different from Jeremiah but who shared his conviction that God would destroy Jerusalem for the disobedience of its people. Those who heard these two prophets refused to accept their message at first. As events bore out the truth of what they were saying, however, people began to accept at least a part of what Jeremiah and Ezekiel said. They became aware of the evils they had committed and the opportunities which they had overlooked. They looked to the future with foreboding. They were overwhelmed with guilt and despair. They did not hear what Jeremiah and Ezekiel said about turning to God. They assumed that God would have nothing more to do with them.

One reason they felt this way was because of their belief in collective guilt. We show the same belief today when we blame a whole race of people for a few unfortunate experiences we have had with members of that race. I knew of one case where the children of a man indicted for murder were ostracized by their playmates, even though the children had nothing to do with the crime. The people of the Bible often thought in this way; that is why Achan's children, and even his cattle, were destroyed with him as punishment for his crime (Joshua 7). In the time of Jeremiah and Ezekiel, there was a widespread feeling that the people of Judah were being punished for the sins of their ancestors as well as for their own. If so, it would do little good to repent. What the fathers had done was past history and could not be changed. The people repeated an old proverb: "The fathers have eaten sour grapes, and the children's teeth are set on edge" (Ezek. 18:2). It was a cry of despair!

Ezekiel tried to combat this feeling of helplessness by rejecting the idea of collective guilt. Speaking for God, he said, "All souls are mine . . . the soul that sins shall die" (18:4). That sounds a bit frightening to us, but it was intended as a word of encouragement. The people who first heard it believed that not only the sinner but everyone connected with him would die. Ezekiel was saying that *only* the soul that sins shall die. In the eighteenth chapter of his book, Ezekiel poses four hypothetical situations and explains how they will be resolved. If there is a good man who obeys God, he will live. Suppose he has a son who turns out badly, will he be able to benefit from his father's righteousness? Not at all—he will be punished for his own sin. Suppose this bad man himself has a son who decides to do what is right. Will God hold him responsible for what his father failed to do? Not at all— he will be rewarded for his own goodness. This was an entirely new idea for the people of Judah and for the exiles in Babylon. The prophet was trying to tell them to forget about the sins of their fathers which had brought such disaster on the nation. They could lead a different life and thereby find a new and vital relationship to God. God would not curse and reject them because of their parents' guilt.

But the people were still not able to lift up their heads. When they looked at their own lives, they found much of which to be ashamed. How could God accept them into his presence when they did not have clean hands and a pure heart? Ezekiel told them that if they turned from evil and did what was right, their past evil deeds would not be held against them. Similarly, if they turned to evil after being righteous, they would not benefit from past goodness. What Ezekiel was trying to do was to *liberate* his countrymen. He wanted to set them free—free from the guilt of their parents, free from their own past mistakes, free from the illusions which led them to despair. He wanted them to see that the future was in their own hands. If they would turn to God in trust, they could find a new and better life.

Jeremiah and Ezekiel were like doctors, trying to deal with a whole nation undergoing a heart attack. They diagnosed the trouble and prescribed medicine. When the people would not accept the advice of these doctors, they suffered severely. At last they were willing to hear what the doctors had been saying. Jeremiah and Ezekiel offered many words of warning that went unheeded. Then, when tragedy came, they offered words of hope. All was not lost if the people would turn to God and accept his guidance.

Recovery Begins: Second Isaiah

Several thousand inhabitants of Judah were taken into exile in Babylon. Those who went first hoped that they would soon return to their homeland, but when Jerusalem fell in 587 B.C. there was little chance of this. The exiles settled down and became adjusted to their new environment. There was time now for reflection on what had happened and why. There was time to ponder what might happen in the future. There were many who saw in the fall of Jerusalem proof that Yahweh, the God of Judah, was unable to protect his people. Others agreed with the prophets that Yahweh had punished his people and then assumed, in spite of the hopes expressed by Jeremiah and Ezekiel, that Yahweh had completely abandoned his people. Some few people among the exiles must have hoped for a better day and looked to Yahweh for forgiveness and help. It was a time for soul-searching and questioning, a time for thinking about the religious meaning of world events.

The Babylonian Empire underwent great upheavals not long after the Jews were taken into exile. A new conqueror appeared, Cyrus the Mede. He gradually gained in power, beginning in 550 B.C. and culminating in control of the whole empire by the year 538. Cyrus seems to have been an enlightened ruler who respected the rights of captive peoples. He saw no need to kill people wholesale and restrained his soldiers from wanton destruction. Cyrus did not, as the Assyrian and Babylonian rulers had done, seek to impose his religion on others. So appealing were his policies that the people of Babylon opened the gates to him and surrendered without a fight. There were many captive groups besides the Jews in the vicinity of Babylon; Cyrus gave them permission to return home and even returned the sacred treasures which had been taken from them. Here was an absolute dictator, to be sure, but one who saw no need to be cruel.

One man among the Jews in Babylon saw here an opportunity to renew his people and return them to their homeland. His name is not known, but his writings are included in the Book of Isaiah and for that reason he is usually called Second Isaiah.[2] Writing about the exciting events and possibilities that accompanied the appearance of Cyrus, he said that God was acting through this man to redeem his people. Though Cyrus did not know it, God was using him as an instrument of salvation for the Jewish people, the prophet said (Isa. 45:1-7).

By reading Isaiah 40 you can grasp most of the important themes in Second Isaiah. The chapter begins with words of reassurance to a people who have accepted the prophets' condemnation. They are well aware of their own sins and the sins of their fathers. But Second Isaiah holds out the gift of God's forgiveness. They have now paid double for all these wrongdoings, and it is time to lift up their heads. The prophet speaks of a highway in the desert by which God will lead his people in triumph back to their homeland. The whole chapter speaks of the power and majesty of God, contradicting the doubts which must have prevailed among the exiles in Babylon. They were quite aware of the power of human empires; the prophet sought to sensitize them to the power of the unseen God. In his eyes the mighty nations are no more than a drop from a bucket (40:15). In the midst of these lofty phrases about the glory of God, the prophet speaks of his tender care for those in need:

> He will feed his flock like a shepherd,
>   he will gather the lambs in his arms,
>   he will carry them in his bosom,
>   and gently lead those that are with young. (40:11)

Against those who contend that God has forgotten them, the prophet argues forcefully. They say, "My way is hid from the LORD, and my right is disregarded by my God" (40:27). The fact is that God cares for them and is able to save them. Second Isaiah expresses this in an unforgettable picture:

> ... they who wait for the LORD shall renew their strength,
> they shall mount up with wings like eagles,
> they shall run and not be weary,
> they shall walk and not faint. (40:31)

Notice that the verbs here are fly—run—walk instead of walk—run—fly. The second order would seem to be logical if one wanted to build toward a climax, but the prophet has seen fit to reverse this order. Was it because he saw that walking steadily may require even more faith than flying?

I always feel frustrated when I speak or write about Second Isaiah because no words of mine can do justice to the exalted language and profound faith which is found in these chapters. These few brief paragraphs will, I hope, encourage you to learn more about them. Let me point to one more of my favorite passages, Isaiah 49:14-18. Here again we find the skepticism which must have pervaded the thinking of the exiles, " 'The Lord has forsaken me, my Lord has forgotten me.' " Can a mother forget her infant? No! Then God cannot forget his people, the prophet asserts. Then he says that the names of the people of Judah are engraved on the palms of God's hands (vs. 16). God cannot forget this people because he has a reminder before his eyes. It is a strange way to speak of God, but it makes the point effectively. Jesus expressed the same truth by saying that the hairs of our heads are all numbered (Matt. 10:30).

The Servant of the Lord

Within the chapters attributed to Second Isaiah are four short poems which have been the subject of much discussion since they were identified by Bernard Duhm in 1892. These are called the "Servant Songs" because they describe the servant of the Lord. They are Isaiah 42:1-4; 49:1-6; 50:4-11; 52:13—53:12. Were all of these written by Second Isaiah? Do they all refer to the same person? Do they refer to a single person or to a group of people? If they refer to a group of people, is it Israel, a remnant of Israelites, the later group known as Christians, or some other group? If the servant is an individual, was it someone who lived before the prophet or someone who came after him? Was it the Messiah, the special leader whom God would send to help his people? All of these possibilities have been suggested at one time or another![3]

I am going to rush in where scholars fear to tread. I will propose a solution to this puzzle which any seminary student can shoot full of holes but which satisfies my own craving to know what happened. With this disclaimer and word of caution, let us proceed.

Among the Jewish exiles by the River Chebar lived a man who was very ill. His disease may have been elephantiasis or leprosy. His flesh was scarred and discolored. His eyes protruded. Great boils on his body gave forth stinking emissions. His breath was foul. His hair was falling out. Some of his flesh dropped off, and a few of his fingers were missing.

None of this man's friends would come near him. Even his own family turned him out. This was the usual treatment of suffering people in biblical times, for illness was regarded as a punishment for sin. That is why Jesus so often said, "Your sins are forgiven," whenever he healed someone. The sick man among the exiles was cut off from the normal consolations of society. People turned their heads to avoid seeing him and walked the other way. No one listened to his story or offered to help him. People thought of him as a sinner. What did he think of himself? It would be strange if he did not share their point of view. In chapter 4 we saw how Job challenged the common belief that suffering is a punishment for sin, but his story is an exception.

How would you react to unspeakable suffering, especially if you believed that God was responsible for what had happened to you? You would probably become bitter. You would wish you had never been born. You would come to hate everyone around you, even members of your own family. You might even curse God. You might question his wisdom or his power to save. You might doubt that God knows the meaning of justice.

This is exactly what did not happen in the case of our sick friend. He did not show any signs of self-pity. Through his disfigured face there gleamed a smile of hope. He did not complain. When mocking children threw stones at him, he did not turn to scowl at them. When the town rascals snatched at his straggling beard, he did not resist them. He said nothing and did nothing to resist. No one knew what the sick man was thinking or how he felt, but it was apparent that he bore no grudge against anyone. He showed no signs of anger, no desire for revenge. When he died, he was cast into a common grave used for criminals and paupers. There his already-decaying body became the food of vultures and maggots. No one seemed to notice or to mourn his passing.

But one person did notice this man—the prophet whom we have called Second Isaiah. Like Jeremiah observing the potter, this prophet saw something in this sick man which disclosed to him the purposes of God. As he watched the tottering and dejected figure, Second Isaiah thought about the tottering and disheartened people to whom he ministered. They had suffered for their sins, but they seemed to have received far more than they really deserved. They had not been as uncomplaining as this brave man! What would happen if they tried to be as forgiving and as strong as he had been? What would happen if they bore their suffering nobly? Could they possibly turn all that anguish into a force for good?

Second Isaiah believed that the people of Judah could bring good out of evil. They were not only bearing their own sin but the sin of other nations as well. What happened to them was not just their own fault, as some of the earlier prophets implied. Edom and Moab and Egypt and Babylon, in varying degrees, were also responsible for what happened. The prophet imagines these nations looking at suffering Judah and saying, "Surely he has borne our griefs and carried our sorrows . . . he was wounded for our transgressions, he was bruised for our iniquities; upon him was the chastisement that made us whole." Through these strange events in which a little nation suffered far more than it deserved, other nations would be led to recognize their own shortcomings. Through humble confession of sin, the whole world could be led to peace. So the seemingly cruel and meaningless suffering of Judah could lead to something of lasting value to the whole world. Such was the prophet's vision, one that began with the actual experiences of a single sick man but quickly led the prophet to dream of what might happen to a whole people if they could be led to understand their situation properly.

Second Isaiah bequeathed to mankind an idea which quickly broke out of its original parameters. It was like a genie coming out of a bottle and becoming something quite different from what the bottle's owner intended. Jesus pondered these "Servant Songs" and used them as a guide for his life. He saw what even his closest disciples could not understand—that one may serve God and fulfill his purposes by humbly accepting suffering and even death. Second Isaiah did not predict the work of Jesus in the sense that he foresaw all that Jesus would do. But he did set forth a concept which Jesus accepted and applied to himself. Jesus rightly saw in these writings the guidance of God for his own life. But the picture in Second Isaiah did not exactly fit Jesus, for there is no record that Jesus was disfigured (Isa. 52:14; 53:2).

Who was the servant of the Lord? My answer is that the idea began with a sick man who accepted his fate bravely and without recrimination. The descriptions in the Servant Songs are so vivid that a living model is highly likely. Second Isaiah was led by this example to write some moving words about suffering and the way in which it might lead to penitence and peace. Jesus took up these magnificent words and attempted to fulfill at least part of their content. We today can find still other meanings in the Servant Songs. We can decide to be a servant people ourselves, accepting evil when it comes to us and attempting to deal with it in creative ways. We may redeem the world from warfare by breaking the vicious cycle of hatred—by responding with forgiveness instead of anger when our rights are compromised. We ourselves can choose to be servants of the Lord.

How did the exiles respond to the message of Second Isaiah? I would like to say that they rose as one person and went back to Judah in triumph, but such was not the case. There are few historical records from this period, but these indicate no sudden return. Only a handful of people returned, and the rest chose to remain in Babylon, where a community of Jews flourished for many centuries. Almost twenty years after Second Isaiah, Haggai complained that the Temple had still not been rebuilt. When the foundation was finally laid, the small size in comparison with the former building caused the old people to groan in dismay (Ezra 3:12). When Nehemiah came to Jerusalem, almost a century after Second Isaiah, the walls of the city had still not been rebuilt.

In terms of their effect on history, then, the words of Second Isaiah were empty. Measured by their beauty and religious significance, however, they are without parallel anywhere. They are certainly the high point of the Old Testament, and they surpass in beauty much of the New Testament as well. Second Isaiah depicts a God who is boundless in power and plenteous in mercy. He is the Ruler of all the nations, but he has a special mission for the people of Judah. Faith and insight are found in these chapters which can still inspire us today.

Judah's hundred-year heart attack triggered a broad range of feelings: complacency, terror, dismay, despair, sober reflection, and chastened optimism. The prophets carried on an argument with the people as a whole—first against their headlong pursuit of policies that could only lead to disaster and then against their dogged refusal to believe in the future and try to change it. The troubles of this crowded century distilled some of the greatest words ever recorded, whether we judge them from a literary point of view or in terms of their religious value. For expressions of the agony which the people of Judah experienced, read Lamentations 2 and 4. For the feelings of those who were carried into exile, read Psalm 137. For a fine description of the whole period discussed in this chapter, I would suggest *A History of Israel* by John Bright (Westminster, 1959), pp. 288-355.

Chapter 7

A Guide
to Reading the Gospels

We could easily spend the major part of our time for Bible study with the four Gospels. They present the center of the Bible message; everything else seems secondary and explanatory. Much in the Gospels can be easily understood. Most of what is found in them is highly interesting. Though many of us have read these stories since childhood, we still enjoy pondering them again. As we try to understand the Gospels, the scholar can help us to a degree. However, there is much that we must do ourselves in order to get inside the Gospels.

To understand the Gospels, we need to know something about how they came to be written. Intensive study of this subject has taken place in the last two centuries. One idea that once prevailed was that Matthew was written first and that Mark was an abridgment of Matthew. This explanation was long ago rejected in favor of the belief that Mark is the earliest of the Gospels. Most scholars now agree that it was written about four decades after the crucifixion of Jesus.

The writer of Matthew made use of Mark and also another written source called Q (from the German *Quelle,* which means "Source"). Besides Mark and Q, the writer of Matthew must have had access to other sources, written and oral. The writer of the Gospel of Luke also made use of Mark and Q, and this writer also used other sources, some of which were perhaps unknown to the writer of Matthew. Thus the first three Gospels were related as shown here:

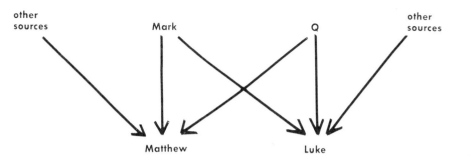

The Gospel of John is quite different from the other three. There is still much uncertainty and discussion regarding it, but many scholars now date it in the last decade of the first century. A good source for further information about the origin of the Gospels is found in an article titled, "The Growth of the Gospels" by Alfred M. Perry in *The Interpreter's Bible,* Vol 7, pp. 60-74.

If you are serious about studying the Gospels, I would suggest your purchasing *Gospel Parallels* edited by Burton H. Throckmorton (Nelson, 1957). I have worn out four copies of this book in twenty-five years. It arranges the material of the first three Gospels in parallel columns for easy comparison, using the *Revised Standard Version.* There are also a good many books on the life and teachings of Jesus. One readable book I would recommend is *The Mind of Jesus* by William Barclay (Harper and Row, 1961).

In this chapter we will select only a few brief passages from the Gospels and approach them in a way that I have found helpful. About each passage there are a few important facts that you need to know. I have given these in a paragraph headed *Explanation.* In the following paragraph, titled *For You to Decide,* I show you how to come to your own conclusions, based on the facts provided in the first paragraph. About any passage of scripture there is room for discussion and disagreement on some important matters. Some of these have to do with events in biblical times about which our information is incomplete. Some of these debatable matters have to do with the application of biblical truths to your own personal situation—a task which only you are competent to carry out. Approaching these passages in this way should help you to become personally involved in the exciting venture of exploring the four Gospels.

Luke's Preface (Read Luke 1:1-4)

Explanation. Here Luke explains his reasons for writing an account of Jesus of Nazareth. Luke wrote about fifty years after the crucifixion. Many others had written about Jesus by this time, including the writer of Mark. Some of these writings may have been much shorter than our Gospels. Most of them are now lost. Some have been incorporated in the four Gospels now found in the Bible. We do not know the identity of "Theophilus." The fact that he is called "most excellent" suggests a Roman official who might be called on to pass judgment on Christians brought before him. This would explain why Luke is careful to show that Jesus did not challenge the political power of Rome or represent any immediate threat to Roman rule.

For You to Decide. What are some of the reasons that motivated Luke to write a Gospel? Consider these possibilities: (a) God told him to do it; (b) The story of Jesus was in danger of being lost unless someone wrote it down; (c) Earlier accounts were not very well organized and were unsatisfactory to Luke; (d) Luke wanted to correct some errors in previous accounts; (e) Luke wanted to emphasize some points about Jesus which he felt were being neglected by other writers. Read the preface to Luke again, and rank these reasons according to their probable importance for Luke, as you now see it. After you have studied the Gospel again, you may have other insights about Luke's motives. Each of the Gospel writers had special reasons for writing. If we can grasp some of these, we can better understand what they have written.

Writing a Gospel (Read John 20:30-31 and 21:25)

Explanation. The word "sign" in the Gospel of John refers to a mighty act or miracle which reveals the presence of God. This Gospel puts great emphasis on discovering who Jesus is and on responding to him in faith. As is the case with any individual about whom we might write a book, the writer could not tell everything that Jesus said and did. In the scripture noted here, the writer says that he has selected what to write with a view to his central purpose—to guide persons toward faith and salvation.

For You to Decide. Why did the writer decide to include the story of Nicodemus, of the woman at the well, of the raising of Lazarus? Why did he fail to tell one single parable of Jesus? Why does he make no direct reference to Jesus' baptism or to the institution of the Lord's Supper? Why did he decide to say nothing about Jesus' temptation experiences? Perhaps the answer to the last question is that he felt these showed Jesus in a bad light. Do you think they do?

Jesus in the Synagogue (Read Luke 4:16-22)

Explanation. When did Jesus' cool reception in his home synagogue take place? Luke 4:23 mentions some things he had previously done at Capernaum, suggesting that it took place after Jesus had been ministering for some time. Matthew and Mark, in fact, put this incident much later than Luke does. The order of events as described in the Gospels is somewhat arbitrary and varies from one Gospel to another. Luke apparently shifted the incident to the very beginning because it showed something fundamental about Jesus' whole ministry: He came to help people, but many of them refused to accept his help.

This incident shows that Jesus attended the synagogue regularly and that he was familiar with the Old Testament Scriptures. When asked to read a passage, he selected a portion of the Book of Isaiah and applied it to himself. The first three Gospels all mention Jesus' teaching in the synagogue, but only Luke describes the content of what he taught.

For You to Decide. What are some ways in which Jesus today proclaims release to captive persons? Does he (a) give oppressed persons the courage to stand up for their rights; (b) set people free from worry about earthly losses by telling them about heaven; (c) help persons free themselves from sinful habits and the remorse which accompanies them; or (d) foster freedom by encouraging those who hold power to treat persons with respect and concern? Decide which two of these four you would consider to be the most significant ways in which Jesus sets persons free. What are some ways in which your freedom is limited? How can Jesus help you to be free?

The Man with the Withered Hand (Read Mark 3:1-6)

Explanation. There are some admirable aspects of sabbath observance by the ancient Jews. Several times they were overcome by their enemies because they refused to fight on the holy day. Such restraint requires conviction and dedication. The Jews understood that there is something holy about rest; it may be just as pleasing in God's sight as the feverish activity we so often offer him instead. The Jews also understood what we today often forget, that there are special times which ought to be set apart for special use, for drawing closer to God.

But Jesus felt that the sabbath was being abused when it became merely a negative restraint from doing anything, when it kept people from helping others as well as from doing evil things. This became apparent when Jesus was confronted with a crip-

95

pled man on the sabbath and his enemies watched to see if he would break the religious law which forbade healing or any other kind of work on the holy day.

For You to Decide. Do you think that Jesus considered it unnecessary to keep the sabbath at all? Why didn't he wait until the following day to heal the man? Why was Jesus angry with the people who were watching him (vs. 5)? Most Christians do not observe the sabbath or seventh day of the week, but they honor the first day in memory of Jesus' resurrection. What do you think Christians should do and refrain from doing on the Lord's Day?

Further Explanation. Here is a comparison of two Gospels:

Matthew 12:13-14	Mark 3:5-6
Then he said to the man, "Stretch out your hand." And the man stretched it out, and it was restored, whole like the other. But the Pharisees went out and took counsel against him, how to destroy him.	And he looked around at them with anger, grieved at their hardness of heart, and said to the man, "Stretch out your hand." He stretched it out, and his hand was restored. The Pharisees went out, and immediately held counsel with the Herodians against him, how to destroy him.

First, note the similarity between these brief excerpts. I like to read diaries of persons who participated in the Civil War. It is interesting to compare how two witnesses will describe the same event. They will often quote a general or political leader in substantially the same words. But they do not describe the event in exactly the same words unless one of them copies from the other. Do you think there is evidence in the above quotations that one writer has copied from the other?

Second, note the differences between the two accounts. Matthew has omitted any reference here to the anger of Jesus. Luke in 6:6-11 also omits the anger of Jesus but says that the scribes and Pharisees were "filled with fury." Luke adds that the withered hand was the man's right hand and says that Jesus knew what his enemies were thinking.

For You to Decide. Why did Matthew omit the anger of Jesus? Why did Luke mention that it was the *right* hand that was crippled? Did he have information not available to the others, or did he add this detail in order to improve the story? What does this story tell us about the priorities of Jesus? He was forced to choose between the needs of persons and the observance of religious rituals. He chose the first. How do you choose between these two?

Peter's Confession of Faith

Matt. 16:13-16, 20	Mark 8:27-30	Luke 9:18-21
Now when Jesus came into the district of Caesarea Philippi, he asked his disciples,	And Jesus went on with his disciples, to the villages of Caesarea Philippi; and on the way he asked his disciples,	Now it happened that as he was *praying alone* the disciples were with him; and he asked them,
"Who do men say that *the Son of Man* is?"	"Who do men say that I am?"	"Who do the people say that I am?"
And they said, "Some say John the Baptist, others say Elijah, and others *Jeremiah* or one of the prophets."	And they told him, "John the Baptist; and others say, Elijah; and others one of the prophets."	And they answered, "John the Baptist; but others say, Elijah; and others, that one of the old p r o p h e t s *has risen.*"
He said to them, "But who do you say that I am?" Simon Peter replied, "You are the Christ, *the Son of the living God.*" . . .	And he asked them, "But who do you say that I am?" Peter answered him, "You are the Christ."	And he said to them, "But who do you say that I am?" And Peter answered, "The Christ *of God.*"
Then he *strictly* charged the disciples to tell no one *that he was the Christ.*	And he charged them to tell no one about him.	But he charged and *commanded* them to tell this to no one...

Explanation. In the above comparison, the significant places at which Matthew and Luke differ from Mark are italicized. This event apparently took place after Jesus had been preaching for some time. It seems that they have not even discussed the identity of Jesus before this time (Note that the Gospel of John indicates that Jesus' disciples recognized him as the Messiah immediately: 1:41, 49). Jesus brought up the question by asking what other persons were saying about him. The disciples had heard various rumors. John the Baptist must have been dead by this time, and persons who knew nothing of Jesus before this might have assumed that he was John come back to life. Some thought he was one of the old prophets. Luke clarifies this by adding a phrase: "One of the old prophets *has risen.*" Then Jesus asked the disciples to give their own view of his identity. Peter spoke for them, and there are three different versions of what he said (see text above). All three Gospels indicate that Jesus wanted them to keep their discovery secret.

For You to Decide. Why are there three different versions of Peter's answer? Is it because these three accounts are about three different, though similar, events? Or did the Gospel writers feel free to make changes, even in something as important as Peter's confession of faith?

Why did Jesus want to keep Peter's answer a secret? Was it because (a) Jesus did not want to arouse his enemies and thereby bring about his death before he could finish his work; (b) Jesus did not accept the title "the Christ"; (c) Jesus accepted the title but meant by it something quite different from what most Jews understood by the term; or (d) Jesus wanted people to make up their own minds about his identity and work. How would you express what you yourself believe about Jesus?

The Parable of the Laborers in the Vineyard (Read Matthew 20:1-16)

Explanation. An allegory is a story in which each character and each feature of the story symbolizes something. Each detail in the allegory of *Pilgrim's Progress* symbolizes some aspect of the Christian life. In a parable, on the other hand, there is a single point which can usually be summarized in one sentence. The other details in the story are merely incidental and should not be "milked" for hidden meanings.

What is the point of this story in Matthew? The last line would seem to explain the story, but it does not really explain the story. Instead of a reversal of fortunes there is an equality of rewards among the laborers. There is evidence that here and elsewhere in the Gospels the last line has been added by someone who thought he understood the point of the story but actually did not. What do you think the point of the story is?

For You to Decide. Read this scripture again and decide which of these statements best summarizes what Jesus was trying to say through this parable: (a) God can do anything he chooses to do; (b) God gives us more than we deserve; (c) An employer should treat all his employees alike; (d) We should not be jealous of other persons; (e) God treats everyone equally; or (f) Those who enter the Kingdom last get as much as those who are in it from the beginning. Read Luke 15:11-32, the parable of the prodigal son. How is it like, and unlike, the parable of the laborers in the vineyard?

Jesus and the Woman at the Well (Read John 4:1-42)

Explanation. This narrative is typical of several encounters between Jesus and various persons in John. Notice that Jesus has no difficulty conversing with the woman of Sychar, even though she is a woman and belongs to a group that is hated by the Jews. But Jesus has difficulty making himself understood. When he speaks of "living water," she insists on taking his words literally. She thinks Jesus is talking about the kind that satisfies our physical thirst. Like Nicodemus in chapter 3, the woman does not grasp the symbolic language of Jesus. When she discovers that Jesus is a prophet, she asks about the proper place to worship. Jesus replies that the manner of worshiping is more important than the place. At last the woman and the other residents of Sychar recognize Jesus as the Christ, the Savior of the world.

For You to Decide. What is meant by the "living water" which Jesus offers to the woman? How do we worship God "in spirit and in truth"? Make a list of acts of worship which you feel are unsatisfactory and unacceptable to God. List some worship experiences which you feel to be satisfactory and acceptable to God. Which of the following probably represent worship which is "in spirit and truth"? An invocation at a public meeting, a prayer in someone's home, a White House prayer breakfast, a folk music worship service, a Christmas oratorio, a brief prayer by a traveler as he or she drives along the highway, an elaborate church wedding, a baptismal service in a country stream, a mass with incense and robed celebrants.

Paying Tribute to Caesar (Read Mark 12:13-17)

Explanation. This is one of several instances when enemies of Jesus tried to trap him by asking a question that is difficult to answer without offending someone. Newspersons do the same thing today in a Presidential press conference. Jesus was asked if the Jews should pay taxes to Caesar. If he answered yes, he would offend the people. If he said no, he would be guilty of treason and would get into trouble with the Roman authorities. Jesus asked to see the money on which Caesar's head was shown. He told his hearers to pay Caesar what was due to him and to give to God what was owed to him.

For You to Decide. Which of these statements best expresses what Jesus meant when he said, "Render to Caesar the things that are Caesar's, and to God the things that are God's"?

1. There are two distinct areas in life, a physical and a spiritual; we should serve Caesar or the government in physical matters and serve God in spiritual or religious matters.

2. We should do what the government requires of us first; then we should do what God requires, if possible.

99

3. We should do what God requires of us first; then we should do what the government requires if it does not conflict with what God requires.

4. Jesus did not really answer the question.

The Parable of the Good Samaritan (Read Luke 10:25-37)

Explanation. The two best parables of Jesus are found only in Luke. The parable of the prodigal son deals with our relationship to God. The parable of the good Samaritan deals with our relationship to other persons. Note that the first two persons who encountered the injured man were religious officials. Neither of them offered to help. The third man was probably a layman and a member of a despised group from the point of view of the Jews. In Luke this parable appears after a lawyer asks Jesus, "Who is my neighbor?" The parable does not really answer this question but another one: How can I be a neighbor? Since the lawyer's question appears in another context in Matthew and Mark, it is suggested that it did not originally belong with the parable.

For You to Decide. What does the commandment "Love thy neighbor" mean? Who are our neighbors? How do we show love for them? Think of some reasons that the priest and the Levite left the man alone and passed on the other side. Why did the Samaritan stop to help the man? What does the parable say to us? Decide which of the following best states what the parable teaches: (a) If you happen to be on the road from Jerusalem to Jericho, be on the watch for victims of robbers; (b) Watch for people in need of help wherever they happen to be; (c) In deciding whether or not to help someone, pay no attention to the person's race, class, nationality, or religion; (d) Give to everyone who asks for help and even to those who need help but don't ask; (e) Be more sensitive to the hurts and concerns of other persons than most of us usually are.

The Parable of the Pounds (Read Luke 19:11-27)

Explanation. Matthew has a parable which appears to be a variant of this one (25:14-30). In Matthew's story, the servants receive the equivalent of $5,000, $2,000, and $1,000. In Luke's version, they all receive $20. The original parable seems to have focused on the timid servant who put his $20 away and did nothing with it. By guarding it carefully, he failed to do what his master required. It is not enough simply to preserve what God gives to us. We must use and multiply it, or we will lose it.

For You to Decide. God gives us many things: the world we live in, life itself, shelter, food, clothing, friends, hope. Think about these three important things that God gives, and decide how we may fail to make the best use of them: (a) *Time.* Everybody has time. If we think we have no time, it simply means we have failed to organize our time properly. We let events and responsibilities control us instead of mastering them. Persons in their youth may have as much as fifty years, or more than 18,000 days ahead of them. How will they use this gift of God for maximum benefit to themselves and others? (b) *Abilities.* Paul speaks in 1 Corinthians of the many gifts which God gives to persons. Some can lead. Some can teach. Some can make things with their hands. Some can sing. Some can write. How do we use our abilities for maximum benefit to ourselves and others? (c) *Faith.* Through our parents and others, God has passed on to us the good news about Jesus Christ. Our faith gives us direction when we are undecided about what to do, and it gives us the power to do what is right. Our faith reassures us in times of uncertainty and danger. Yet we can fail to make use of this gift of God and thereby lose it. We may take our faith for granted and assume that it will be available when we really need it, even though we have not examined or used it in the meantime. We may find, however, that faith disappears when neglected. Those who talk with others about what they believe and do not believe, who try to understand who God is and what he expects of us, who practice the faith through prayer and service, find that their faith grows and becomes more and more effective.

The Parable of the Last Judgment (Read Matthew 25:31-46)

Explanation. This is one of my favorite passages because it has so many thought-provoking aspects and because I continually see in it meanings I had not seen before. The "Son of man" probably refers to a heavenly figure who was to appear and judge mankind at the end of the age, according to Jewish literature. It is possible that Jesus identified himself as the Son of man. In the parable, those who are judged fall into two categories, the "sheep" and the "goats." The sheep are said to have performed simple acts of mercy and in doing this to have served the Son of man or the King. The goats, on the other hand, neglected opportunities to serve by doing simple acts of mercy. Both the good and the evil persons were surprised when they heard the verdict of the Son of man regarding their lives.

For You to Decide. Is this story primarily about the future, or is it about what is happening in our lives right now? How much of the story is symbolic, and how much of it is to be taken literally? What are some acts which we might do today in order to be like the sheep? Does the story mean that true goodness is something we do without thinking about it as deserving a reward? Does the story mean "Be like the sheep"? But the sheep did not consciously try to be like that!

Washing the Disciples' Feet (Read John 13:1-15)

Explanation. The Gospel of Luke supplies these words of Jesus: "Let the greatest among you become as the youngest, and the leader as one who serves. For which is the greater, one who sits at table, or one who serves? Is it not the one who sits at table? But I am among you as one who serves." (22:26f.) It has been suggested that the story of Jesus' washing the disciples' feet, given only by the Gospel of John, is an elaboration of these words in Luke. Jesus demonstrates what he means by accepting a humble position of service instead of seeking a place of honor and influence. The story skillfully summarizes what Jesus' whole life was all about. In the words of Paul, he "emptied himself, taking the form of a servant" (Phil. 2:7).

For You to Decide. What is the connection between John 13:3 and 13:4? Verse 3 says that Jesus knew three things: that God had given him all things, that he came from God, and that he was going to God. What did this knowledge have to do with his washing the disciples' feet? (a) Jesus knew that his time was short, and he wanted to leave his disciples with a vivid object lesson before leaving them. (b) Only insignificant people have to demand their rights. Jesus knew that he was important and could freely give himself without fearing loss of status. (c) The two verses show the two sides of Jesus' character in the Gospel of John. He is the Word of God who has become flesh and has dwelt among us. Which of these three best expresses the relationship between 13:3 and 13:4?

Exploring the Teachings of Jesus

The teachings of Jesus lend themselves to endless exploration. As we ponder them, we gain helpful insights into the character of Jesus, the ordering of our life together, and the concern which God has for each of us. In the following paragraphs I have given some important questions along with some scripture references to which you may turn in order to discover your own answers to them. Read the scriptures suggested and try to answer the questions in each paragraph. After you have tried to find your own answers, you may want to consult a Bible dictionary or *The Mind of Jesus* by William Barclay (Harper & Row, 1961) to see what others have concluded about these questions.

The Kingdom of God or the Kingdom of Heaven. Where is it located? See Matt. 8:11; 16:19; 26:29; Luke 17:20-21; John 18:36. Does it come now, or later? Matt. 4:17; 6:10; 12:28; Luke 4:43; 9:27; 10:9; 17:20-21. What is the kingdom like? Matt. 13:24-30, 31-33, 44-46. Who may enter the kingdom? Matt. 5:3, 10, 19, 20; 7:21; 18:4; 19:14; Mark 9:47; Luke 6:20; 9:62; 18:24-25; John 3:3, 5.

The Nature of God. Does God care about what happens to persons? Does he answer our prayers? Does he try to catch us in wrongdoing in order to punish us? Does he forgive all our sins, with no strings attached? See Matt. 7:7-11; 20:1-16; 22: 1-14; Luke 6:32-38; 11:5-8; 14:15-24; 15:1-32; 18:1-8.

Jesus' Conception of Himself. Did Jesus claim to be the Messiah? Did he try to keep his identity a secret? If so, why? What role did Jesus accept for himself? What roles did he reject? See Matt. 3:13-17; 4:1-11; 20:20-28; Mark 3:11-12; Luke 4:16-30; 9:18-36; John 1:35-51; 4:25-26; 10:24-25; 18:33-38.

Jesus' Teaching About Prayer. What attitudes in prayer did Jesus condemn? What attitudes and words did he commend? Did he say that all prayers would be answered? Matt. 6:5-15; Luke 11:9-13.

Forgiveness. Under what conditions should we forgive persons who have injured us? Can we expect to be forgiven if we do not forgive others? Matt. 18:23-35; Mark 11:25-26; Luke 17:3-4.

Marriage and Divorce. How did Jesus understand the institution of marriage? Were there any circumstances under which he permitted divorce? It there a difference among the gospels on this teaching? How do you explain it? See Matt. 5:31-32; 19:1-12; Mark 10:1-12; Luke 16:18.

Jesus' Reason for Healing the Sick. Why did Jesus heal persons? Was it because of his compassion for them or because he wanted to show what he could do? Is there any difference among the four Gospels in their description of Jesus' healings? Matt. 8:1-17; 9:32-34; 20:29-34; Mark 2:1-12; Luke 6:6-11; 14:1-6; 17:11-19; John 5:1-18; 9:1-41.

Jesus' Teaching About the Future. Did Jesus expect the end of the world in his own lifetime? Did he expect it to happen soon after his crucifixion? What did he warn his disciples to get ready for? What does this teaching of Jesus say to us today? See Matt. 10:23; 16:28 and chapters 24—25. See Acts 1:1-11.

Chapter 8

The Bondage of Perfect Freedom: Galatians

Flood waters threatened an Arkansas town. All able-bodied persons were mustered to fill sandbags and try to shore up the levee. Saturday night the Corps of Engineers reported the river would crest Sunday afternoon and that the town could be saved if everyone helped. A group gathered around one of the ministers, who was shoveling sand, to decide what to do. Many were not in favor of working on Sunday, even if the town were flooded. Some even suggested that if they all went to church and prayed, God would save the town by a miracle. The minister counseled the people to adapt their religious practice to the present emergency.

"Paul wrote in Galatians," he said, " 'For freedom Christ has set us free.' "

One of the church elders thought about that for a time and then said, "I've been meaning to say something about Paul that has always troubled me. Don't you think, preacher, that he was a dangerous radical?"

The Theme of Galatians

Did Paul really mean what he said about our freedom in Christ? The statement quoted by the Arkansas minister was not a casual remark of Paul but is the theme of all six chapters of the Letter to the Galatians. Paul felt so strongly that his feelings about it still radiate from the printed pages of our New Testaments. Is it possible that Paul carried his passion for freedom too far? Many persons who knew him personally, both Jews and Christians, thought so. Many Christians today are unwilling to give themselves or others the kind of liberty that Paul commended. Many have rather definite ideas about what Christians may do and may not do. All of us could profit from an investigation of

Paul's idea of Christian freedom. It is an important and meaningful concept, but it has often been misunderstood.

The Letter to the Galatians presents the gospel as Paul proclaimed it. It summarizes what Paul taught in his preaching and in his other letters. At the same time, it tells us much about Paul as a person. We find him locked in a great struggle for the souls of his Galatian friends, believing that their eternal destiny hinged on the outcome of this fight. Paul is no armchair theologian in this letter, speculating about what may or may not be true. He is a soldier armed for spiritual warfare, and he gives the enemy no quarter! While in other letters Paul demonstrated a remarkable amount of tolerance for those who disagreed, in Galatians he thundered against ideas and practices which he could not condone. We see that he was a person who had strong emotions, and we discover what he found to be utterly intolerable.

The drama began when Paul preached to the Gentiles in Galatia some time before the letter was written. Paul simply told them of the love of God in Christ, and they responded gladly. They were baptized into the Christian fellowship and received the Holy Spirit.

Then Paul went on to other cities, and other Christian preachers came to visit the new converts at Galatia. These are called Judaizers because they believed that Christians needed to continue some of the practices of the Jewish religion. It may be that these preachers followed Paul for the express purpose of correcting what they considered to be deficiencies in his missionary work. The Judaizers told the Galatians that they needed to practice circumcision and observe some Jewish holy days which Paul had neglected to mention. They told the Galatians that Paul was not really an apostle, since he had not been one of the original disciples of Jesus and had not known Jesus in the flesh.

When Paul heard about this visit of the Judaizers and the fact that the Galatians accepted their arguments, he was furious. The language he used to express his anger is almost unprintable, and most translations soften it somewhat. Paul cursed his opponents (1:9). The point of his remark in 5:12 is: If these men see so much virtue in shortening the male penis, why not go the whole way, beginning with their own? This is shocking language for a Christian preacher, not only because of its indelicacy but also because of the attitude it displays toward persons who were, after all, human beings. The only explanation I can give is that Paul felt unusually provoked by what these Judaizers had done to the religious life of his Galatian friends. They had not simply supplemented his careful work; Paul believed they had destroyed it.

It does seem strange that Paul reacted so angrily, especially when it seems apparent that the Judaizers only suggested a few additions to what Paul had taught the Galatians. But for Paul these changes were critical; they changed the very nature of the gospel he had preached. Paul called it a new kind of bondage. He had found the Galatians enslaved to superstition and fear of demons, the "elemental spirits." Paul had set these persons free by attaching them to the Lord Jesus Christ, who is stronger than all such spirits. Now they had surrendered to a new kind of bondage—not to demons but to Jewish religious practices.

Paul's revolt against the religion of his youth was almost total. Whereas he had passionately defended it at one time, he now saw it as utterly false. We have to guard against viewing first-century Judaism through the eyes of Paul. Judaism was much more than simply the punctilious observance of meaningless rules. For a long time there was uncertainty, even among Christians, about whether the church was a continuation of Judaism or not. Even when it finally broke away, the church inherited much from the Jews. Leaders like James, Peter, and Barnabas were unwilling to go as far as Paul in rejecting the Jewish heritage.

One aspect of early Judaism does seem hard for me to accept. The volume on the sabbath in the Babylonian Talmud has fascinated me, but its hair-splitting legalism is beyond my comprehension. In it the command to remember the sabbath day is taken to a point of absurdity. The sabbath begins at sundown, but what is the precise time? Answer: When one can see two stars. No food is to be prepared after that moment; food for the sabbath must be prepared the day before. But what if one has a loaf of bread in the oven, and it is still baking when the sabbath arrives? At what point can the process of baking be said to end, so that one can avoid having it take place on the sabbath? When the crust is formed? On all sides of the loaf or just part of it? And so on. My exasperated question is: What possible interest can the Lord of the universe have in such fine distinctions? And what if one succeeds, by great thought and care, in keeping the sabbath? Does this assure that one will have a meaningful relationship with God?

Justification by Faith

Concern about keeping the sabbath and other Jewish rules once appealed to Paul. If he kept such rules after becoming a follower of Christ, it was for an entirely different reason. He saw no reason to burden his Gentile converts with them. In fact, he saw danger in their accepting even the simple rite of circumcision. It implied a trust in what they could do to make themselves ac-

106

ceptable to God rather than grateful response to the free gift of God's love in Christ.

For all the dramatic change that took place in Paul when he accepted Christ as Lord, one thing remained the same. Before and after the experience he was preoccupied with the question: How may a person be acceptable to God? By disobeying God's commands, Paul believed, persons had erected a barrier between themselves and the God who created them. Only by finding their way back to God could they be restored to life and peace. Before his conversion, Paul sought to win God's acceptance by keeping the Ten Commandments, plus all the other commandments by which the Old Testament and Jewish commentators supplemented them. If he could be good enough, Paul reasoned, God would *have to accept him.*

Even if Paul could have kept the commandments (and he found that he could not!), what kind of approach is this for even a good person to make toward God? What right has anyone to tell God what he must do? The gospel of Christ, as Paul understood it, means that we are accepted by God in spite of the fact that we have not kept the rules. If we really accept this gift from God, we will not anxiously try to prove to God that we are good. Effort to do this implies that we lack faith and have not accepted God's gift in Christ. There are thus two ways to relate to God, and we must decide on one or the other:

by obeying rules	by responding in faith
• pride in our own accomplishment	• gratitude for God's gift
• fear of making a mistake	• confidence that we are accepted
• concern about ourselves	• concern about other persons
• being good in order to win God's acceptance	• being good because God has accepted us
• justification by good works	• justification by faith

Paul used Abraham as an example of what he meant by "justification by faith." Revered as the ancestor of the Jews and as a religious pioneer, Abraham knew nothing of the Jewish Law, which was received from God centuries after Abraham. Yet Abraham established a relationship with God which was more than satisfactory. He did this simply by believing God's promises, by responding in faith, not in an anxious effort to prove his own goodness. Paul interpreted Christianity as a return to this simple faith of Abraham. Thus it was not a denial of Judaism but its ful-fillment.

I would suggest that you take time to read the Letter to the Galatians at this point and then read the rest of this chapter.

What Freedom in Christ Means

Augustine, who lived four centuries after Paul, understood what the apostle meant by freedom. Augustine described his own early life as "the freedom which is perfect bondage." It was a time of drifting, of self-indulgence, of physical abuse, and intellectual license. It seemed like freedom, but this was an illusion; for Augustine was enslaved to passion and false ideas. When Augustine found Jesus Christ, he accepted the Savior as Lord. Now he was in bondage to Christ, but he experienced freedom for the first time. He said that he went from the freedom that is perfect bondage to the bondage that is perfect freedom.

All of us want freedom, but few of us know what the word means. Various forms of slavery offer themselves to us as genuine freedom. I recall a young man whose father had decided on his college course and subsequent career. The youth had nothing against this career except that he had not chosen it himself. He deeply resented his father's gentle but firm control. Unable to express this resentment or to make his father understand, he signed up for four years in the Air Force. The young man explained this action to me as a way of obtaining his freedom, but I saw it as simply the substitution of one form of bondage for another. As long as the youth's behavior was determined by the need to rebel against his father, he would not be free. I proposed that the whole family go through the painful but necessary process of thinking through their relationships under the guidance of a counselor. This would enable them to understand and control the forces which drove them to do irrational and destructive things to each other.

Claude Steiner has written a helpful book titled *Scripts People Live* (Grove Press, Inc., 1974). According to Steiner, we all follow scripts given to us long ago, mainly by our parents. Conflict within us results from the fact that one parent gave us one script, and the other parent gave us another. Often the same parent may give conflicting scripts. We are set free, Steiner suggests, when we examine the scripts we have received from others and choose to write our own.

Paul proposed a different solution. He said that freedom comes when we allow Christ to write our script, when Christ controls our lives. If Christ does not control us, someone else less desirable will. The person who stands alone is not free. He or she is vulnerable to every conceivable influence from outside. Only with the strength Christ gives us can we withstand these forces. Only in his power can we be free.

Being controlled by Christ does not mean joining a narrow religious sect or accepting the teachings of some leader who claims to represent Christ. It does not mean, Paul made clear, settling into a dull conformity with the thinking and behavior of others who call themselves Christian. Paul found a remarkable variety of life-styles among those who belonged to Christ, and he rejoiced. "For freedom Christ has set us free," he wrote, "stand fast, therefore, and do not submit again to a yoke of slavery" (Gal. 5:1).

In Galatians 5, Paul wrote that we must choose between the flesh and the Spirit. The word "flesh" evokes images of physical appetites and sensual indulgence. But Paul used the word to mean much more than this. Some ancient thinkers saw human life as a struggle between flesh and spirit, meaning by the former such human appetites as hunger and sex. Salvation comes, they said, when we control the physical appetites and cultivate the intellect and spirit. But Paul makes clear that flesh includes all kinds of selfish behavior: "enmity, strife, jealousy, anger, selfishness, dissension, party spirit, envy" (5:20-21). Many of the works which Paul associated with flesh were actions and attitudes which lead to a breakdown in human relationships. In this sense it is possible for religious and "spiritual" people to be of the flesh. In fact, the Judaizers were following the flesh when they used religious practices to promote themselves. If following rules tends to separate us from other Christians and makes us feel superior, then we belong to the flesh. This explains why Paul wrote: "Do not use your freedom as an opportunity for the flesh, but through love be servants of one another" (5:13).

The Spirit enables us to serve one another. It brings persons together. It teaches "love, joy, peace, patience, kindness, faithfulness, gentleness, self-control (5:22-23). If we think we have the Spirit and yet are unable to relate to other Christians, it is not the Spirit of Christ that we possess. We are, in that case, still dominated by the flesh. The only way to escape domination by the flesh is to submit to the Spirit. Paul emphasizes that the Spirit will lead us away from self-conceit and envy. The Spirit brings Christians together. The kind of thing that was happening in the Galatian churches, where some members embraced practices that made them feel superior to other members, really divides the church and has done so through twenty centuries.

Paul saw the Spirit of Christ as a power that works in an amazing variety of ways. First Corinthians 12—14 is a brilliant essay on the amazing number of ways in which the Spirit works among Christians. What we have to do is to accept this variety and recognize the presence of the Spirit in others, even though they do not act and think as we do. The Spirit does not destroy individuality but enhances it, much as a good sauce does not mask but brings out the flavor of the meat it garnishes. It was precisely because Christians at Corinth did not understand the Spirit this way that Paul wrote as he did. Like many Christians today, they condemned or pitied those who did not have the same experience of the Spirit as themselves.

The Message of Galatians for Today

The "flood story" with which this chapter began is apocryphal, and the kind of legalism it describes is not a temptation for most persons today. But there are other kinds of legalism and moralism which are, to my mind, even more appalling.

If there is any trait that characterizes our time, it is a sense of sin. Our magazines and newspapers, our radio and television, are full of complaints about what people have done that they ought not to have done. Men have deprived women of their rightful place in the working world. Advertisers have not told the whole truth about their products. Politicians have made promises they had no intention of fulfilling. Parents have been dishonest with their children. Criminals have stolen property and committed brutal murders. Police have abused their power and violated citizens' rights. And all of us have thrown our garbage into Mother Nature's lap for too many years.

I have no quarrel with this analysis of our human predicament. I have helped write some of it myself. I do think we need to look carefully at some of the attitudes which accompany our contemporary sense of sin. Whereas an earlier generation was critical of dancing, card-playing, drinking, and necking, we are alarmed about male chauvinism, racism, crime, political corruption, and economic injustice. The sins we condemn are different, but we regard them in much the same way as our legalistic parents regarded the sins they chose to deplore. Our sins are chiefly things that other persons do. We quickly see what these persons ought to do and are surprised if others do not recognize it as well. In short, we are as smug and self-righteous about sin today as were the Judaizers whom Paul condemned in the Galatian letter.

I want to affirm that women have been abused by our laws, employment practices, advertising, and educational curricula. I think it is high time to allow women to be persons, to choose the role that has meaning for them without having one imposed on them by others. But I am not at all sure what we need to do or stop doing in order to help women. I would like to see more women doctors, administrators, lawyers, and political leaders. I would like to see women be free to become ordained ministers and assume the same leadership roles that are open to men. But I do not see value in changing all references to "mankind" and "man" in our hymns and prayers. Perhaps this is due to my ignorance or chauvinism, or it may simply be an individual difference that others can respect and tolerate. I hope it is!

The national assemblies of our church are held every two years. After the evening sessions of these assemblies, groups of people meet in hotel ballrooms to discuss causes in which they are mutually interested. These include pacifism, church unity, evangelism, the plight of the farmworkers, and (lately) the charismatic movement. The causes are different in these meetings, but the agenda is predictable in each case. It includes mutual encouragement, strategy for promoting the cause, and hours of deploring the others who are not yet enlightened. There is rarely a period scheduled for self-examination or penitence. There is little opportunity to question the basic assumptions which have brought the group together. If someone wanders in who does not share these assumptions, or who shows that he or she is simply uninformed about them, that person usually gets short shrift.

If anyone ever feared that our changing values would result in a kind of amoral society in which anything goes, he (or she!) need have no fear. We are almost obsessed with the idea that things are wrong and that something should be done about them. Our problem is lack of patience with persons who do not perceive the same evils that we perceive or do not advocate the same remedies.

This is not the place to describe what may be done about this tendency to moralism in society as a whole, but I do want to call attention to our Christian heritage of freedom in the Spirit. We Christians ought not to feel smug in our support of the right causes while we berate or barely tolerate our brothers and sisters who do not support them. Paul has shown us that something more is needed besides correct ideas and correct behavior. We need to establish and maintain relationships with God and with our fellow Christians. The Spirit will help us do this if we will allow it to do so.

"Where the Spirit of the Lord is, there is freedom," Paul wrote (2 Cor. 3:17). A valid way to restate this, I believe, is that the

Spirit engenders variety and teaches respect for persons who differ from ourselves. It does not encourage any religious activity or attitude which lulls us into a feeling of satisfaction with ourselves and contempt for those who have had a different experience.

All this is not to suggest that the sins of our time can be safely disregarded or that any opinion about them is as good as any other. War, crime, economic injustice, and oppression of women, to name only a few evils, are real and demand remedy. But while we are seeking remedies, we must deepen our capacity to love. Love in the New Testament is something more than attraction to persons who seem appealing to us and think as we do. Love is genuine concern for those who differ, and it is not just zeal to enlighten and reform such persons.

We need to confront modern moralism with a kind of sophistication which exposes its absurdity. The enlightened person in our time should realize that all moral values are shaped by one's cultural milieu and place in history. We have different ideas of right and wrong because we have different experiences. Many of our strongest convictions are a product of years of struggle and reflection. Yet we display amazement if others do not simply accept our view on our bare suggestion, without anything like the same struggle. Christian freedom implies patience with the apparent "backwardness" of others as well as some healthy skepticism about the finality of our own cherished views. Where the Spirit is, there is humility.

A New Surge of Freedom

Fortunately, there are signs that we can accept and even rejoice in individual differences to a greater degree than formerly. Ten years ago, a beard was a sign of protest; today it means nothing in particular. Women have a number of choices of acceptable clothing styles. These are outward symbols of a deeper respect for diversity—a healthy development which is also found in the church.

I recently attended a church meeting that was different and refreshing. No one stood before the group in order to tell the rest of us what we ought to believe and do. Each person present wrote out a profile of his or her interests and posted it on the wall. Then we all moved around and found persons who could help us learn something we wanted to know or do something we wanted to do. Each participant was free to plan his or her own growing experiences, and there were others ready to help us when we asked. It was an example of genuine liberation.

A few years ago the Protestant churches experienced a liturgical renewal. There was an effort to encourage use of the "proper" vestments, the "proper" colors for each season, and uniformity in orders of worship. Today the watchword is spontaneity and freedom in worship, and almost anything is possible—guitars, tambourines, banners, balloons.

All of this is in keeping with what Paul wrote in Galatians about Christian freedom. Freedom is important because it makes growth possible and because it affirms the worthwhileness of each individual Christian. Freedom is also necessary in order to assure the effective operation of the Spirit. The Spirit can only work through persons who are free to respond to it. The Spirit can only carry out needed reforms when persons are sensitive to its gentle influence. When we become obsessed with the preservation of an institution and its forms, whenever we identify Christianity with bland conformity, we stifle the Spirit and prevent the multitude of experiences it makes possible for Christians who are free.

Freedom in Christ enables persons of divergent views and a variety of life-styles to relate to each other in love. It also makes possible a richly satisfying relationship to God. Too many of us still put our religion on a barter basis. We think God owes us something for supporting his programs, whether we conceive them in terms of personal piety or of social reform. We attempt to bribe God to accept us by making the right choices and supporting the right causes. We measure ourselves by new yardsticks today, but we still measure ourselves. It is hard to believe that God accepts us just as we are, regardless of what we have done or failed to do. It is difficult for us to come to God empty-handed, relying entirely on his love and forgivenes, just as it was hard for the Galatians to come to God in faith.

But if we can discover the freedom made possible by the Spirit, we can discover new depths in our religious life and explore a novel relationship to the God who is revealed in Jesus Christ. We can do right, not in order to win God's favor but because he is already at work in us. We can concentrate on the most effective ways of serving our neighbors instead of worrying endlessly about ethical choices. We can accept our own existence without waiting until we can prove our right to exist. We can rejoice in the unique role which God has made possible for us. Such freedom is not aimless drifting. It is a close relationship to the God who made us, a relationship which alone can rescue us from all those petty slaveries to which we are subject. In the words of Augustine, we have found the bondage that is perfect freedom.

Chapter 9

The Importance
of Remembering:
Deuteronomy

The Broadway musical *Fiddler on the Roof* is about a Jewish community in nineteenth-century Russia. As it begins, the peasant Tevye explains life in Anatevka. "Each of us is like a fiddler on a roof," he says, "we are trying to play a simple melody without falling off and breaking our necks."

When someone asks Tevye how he and his neighbors keep their balance in this precarious position, he answers in one word: *tradition*. The people have traditions that tell them how to sleep, what to eat, when to work, what to wear. "Because of our tradition, each of us knows who he is and what God wants him to do," Tevye explains.

We are a people who have forgotten our traditions, and we are the poorer for it. Few of us can trace our ancestry more than two or three generations. In school we demand courses that will help us get better jobs or provide a usable skill. We have little time for history or for the great ideas of the past. In making decisions, we consult our feelings or perhaps ask the advice of friends. We are not interested in what our grandparents would have done. Tevye admitted that being a fiddler on a roof was difficult. But trying to live without traditions, as we do, is impossible. We do not know who we are or what we should do in order to find and preserve our lives.

A Book that Changed a Nation

The whole Bible is concerned with remembering, preserving, and interpreting traditions, but the part of the Bible which does this best is the Book of Deuteronomy. Based on old memories, Deuteronomy was written in the seventh century B.C. Like other books of the Old Testament, it was edited and supplemented several times in the centuries that followed.

MOSES   DEUTERONOMY   JESUS

1500 B.C.   1000 B.C.   500 B.C.   0   100 A.D.

The manner in which Deuteronomy came to light is described in 2 Kings 22—23. King Josiah, only twenty-six years old, sought to restore the nation of Judah after years of decline. For decades his people had been dominated by the power of Assyria and had adopted the religious practices of that nation and of other nearby peoples. Judah had lost its independence, its self-respect, and its distinctive identity. Josiah sought to change this in several ways. For one thing, he ordered the repair of the temple in Jerusalem, the house of God and the religious center of the nation.

In the process of cleaning and repairing the temple, a book was found. When this was taken to King Josiah, he tore his clothes in anguish because he realized that his people had not obeyed the laws of God set forth in this book. Josiah took the book to the temple and read it in the presence of the people. Then all of them joined in a covenant to obey the words set forth in Deuteronomy.

What the king did is set forth in 2 Kings 23:4-25. He removed from the temple the cult objects which did not belong to Yahweh, Israel's God. He abolished idol worship in the many sanctuaries around Jerusalem, where it had flourished for decades. He destroyed the altar at Bethel, where Amos had preached a century earlier. He suppressed mediums and wizards. And he proclaimed a Passover celebration according to the instructions in the newly-discovered book. Rarely, if ever, has a book had such a profound effect on a whole people. And this was not the end of the matter. A school of interpreters grew up around Deuteronomy, and the effects of their work are to be found in several other parts of the Bible.

115

Deuteronomy appeared at an opportune time. There was a great *need* to recover Judah's past and to reform its religious life. This need was accompanied by a unique *opportunity* brought about by the decline of Assyrian power. Judah was now free to develop in its own way. This need and opportunity were met by a *leader,* Josiah, who seems to have been a sincere and capable young man. For these elements, Deuteronomy provided a fourth essential—a *blueprint* for change.

The changes called for in the new book were far-reaching. Centering worship in the Jerusalem temple meant that many priests were demoted or without work. We can imagine how they felt about such changes. The rules regarding debts and slaves apparently went farther than other codes that we know about, and they must have encountered stiff resistance from the rich and powerful. There were important new elements in the teaching of Deuteronomy, but basically it was a call to return to the original vision which brought Israel into existence. Thus it was both new and old, both radical and conservative.

What Being God's People Means

Thomas Jefferson often spoke of "the Spirit of 1776" and deplored the fact that it had been so easily lost. He meant that Americans seemed to forget the principles on which their nation was founded and the liberties for which the previous generation had fought. To retain the original ideals of America, it was necessary to remember how the nation had come into being and why.

Deuteronomy is in the form of a speech attributed to Moses, in which he calls on the people of Israel to remember their heritage. He speaks as they are about to enter the promised land after forty years in the wilderness, and he notes that they have already begun to forget the experience of slavery in Egypt and the miraculous events which brought their deliverance. Unless they could recover this tradition, all the precious gifts which had been given to them would be lost.

The Book of Deuteronomy emphasizes five essential points which must be remembered by the people of Israel:

1. *They came out of slavery in Egypt.* Again and again this point is made in the book. Even the sabbath became, not a recollection of the Creation as in Exodus, but a reminder of the days of slavery. Israel was to remember this so that she might not become proud and so that she could be understanding toward slaves in her own nation (Deut. 5:12-15). Israel had once known slavery and could enter it again. Parents who have known poverty in childhood are chagrined by the casual way in which their affluent

children spend money. To appreciate what we have, we need a vivid memory of what things were like before our good fortune.

2. *God has intervened to bring them freedom and prosperity.* The details of the deliverance from Egypt, God's guidance in the wilderness forty years, the miraculous gift of manna to eat, and the overcoming of enemies are retold by Deuteronomy so that the readers might not forget what God had done for them. The writer sought to recapture the awe-inspiring experience of God's presence for a people who had become bored with their own traditions. He sought to remind them that they were a special people who had been visited by God in a unique way. They were never to think of themselves as just like any other group (7:6).

3. *They were recipients of God's grace.* There is absolutely no explanation for God's choice of Israel rather than some other people. They were not a numerous people, and God did not choose them because they were better than others or because he saw in them great potential for growth. He helped them because he loved them and because he had made promises to their ancestors. Thus Israel has received God's *grace*—his blessing bestowed on the undeserving. The only possible response to this is humble gratitude. Israel must never take God's gift for granted, for in that moment she will lose it (7:7-11; 8:11-20).

4. *God has given Israel rules that must be obeyed.* One side of the covenant is what God has done for the people which he has chosen. The other side is what they must do for him. The rules given in Deuteronomy are not just abstract principles; they are related to Israel's past and present experience. They are not simply good advice about how to live. They are solemn demands from a God who has every right to require obedience precisely because of what he has done for those who are to obey. This is a kind of "situation ethics" because it is based on the situation of the persons who must choose. The situation, however, is not just what is happening in the present but all that has happened in the past as well. Because of what God has done and who Israel is, she must obey. The Ten Commandments in Deuteronomy 5 are not just ten rules that apply to everyone but ten commands to a people who have been saved; they are valid because they are given by the One who did the saving:

> I am the LORD your God, who brought you out of the land of Egypt, out of the house of bondage. You shall have no other gods before me. You shall not make for yourself a graven image. . . (Deut. 5: 6-8).

5. *The consequences of obedience are life and peace, but the consequence of disobedience is destruction.* Deuteronomy is filled

with dire warnings of what will happen if the commands of God are not obeyed. No wonder King Josiah tore his garments in anguish when he heard these words! The doctrine of retribution is here—Israel will be punished for wrongdoing and rewarded for obedience. But the reward and punishment are both far in excess of what the people do. Obedience will bring blessings beyond imagination, while disobedience will trigger indescribable evils that will persist for generations (28:1-24).

Preserving the Sacred Memories

Deuteronomy might well carry as a motto: "To forget is to perish; to remember is to live." The traditions are to be a basic part of life:

> These words which I command you this day shall be upon your heart; and you shall teach them diligently to your children, and shall talk of them when you sit in your house, and when you walk by the way, and when you lie down, and when you rise. (6:6-7)

But the preservation of holy memories is not simply the perfunctory repetition of empty phrases. It must include a lively description of what God has done for this people so that they may remember that they exist only by his grace. It must include a dramatic reenactment of the experience in the wilderness so that the people will understand why they must obey the commands of God. Deuteronomy 6:20-25 describes how a son may ask about the traditions and be told their meaning in terms which vividly recall the stirring events on which they are based.

Deuteronomy 26:1-11 preserves a ritual which is centuries older than the book itself. Here is an old Israelite worship service, with the creed which was an intrinsic part of that worship. This passage shows that Israel's faith consisted of recitation of God's mighty deeds, a relation of past events which helped the worshiper to understand who he was and what was required of him in the present.

The worshiper brought a basket of the first products of the harvest and gave them to the priest in God's temple. Then he recited the creed:

> A wandering Aramean was my father; and he went down into Egypt and sojourned there, few in number; and there he became a nation, great, mighty, and populous. And the Egyptians treated us harshly, and afflicted us, and laid upon us hard bondage. Then we cried to the LORD the God of our fathers, and the LORD heard our voice, and saw our affliction, our toil, and our oppression; and the LORD brought us out of Egypt with a mighty hand and an outstretched arm, with great terror, with signs and wonders; and he brought us into this place and gave us this land, a land flowing with milk and honey. And be-

hold, now I bring the first of the fruit of the ground, which thou, O Lord, hast given me (Deut. 26:5-10).

Note the following about this important passage:

1. There is a sharp *contrast* between the situation of the worshiper's people when they were nomads and slaves, on the one hand, and after God intervened to help them, on the other hand. Presumably, they would still be enslaved if it had not been for God's help. Their gratitude should reflect the fact that they are utterly dependent on God.

2. The worshiper describes events of the past as though he himself had *participated* in them ("the Egyptians treated *us* harshly"). He is not simply telling something that happened long ago but is describing his own story, one which he has completely appropriated and which has become the basis for his own understanding of himself.

3. The creed speaks of God in terms of *what God does* rather than what he is. We say, "I believe in God the Father, Almighty, Maker of heaven and earth." Much of our theology deals with the nature of God as an eternal reality. But the Hebrew is not interested in abstract speculation about God's nature. He knows God only as a result of what God has done, and it is of this that he speaks so eloquently in Deuteronomy and elsewhere.

4. The worshiper brings a gift as an act of gratitude and also as a *dramatic sign* of participation in Israel's covenant with God. His religion is not simply a matter of words and ideas but involves action as well. It requires a vivid recollection of past events so that they become present realities. It also requires a response on the part of the worshiper and a commitment to serve the God who has done so much for the worshiper and for his people.

Ordering Human Relationships

Many of the laws in Deuteronomy 12—25 seem remote from our contemporary experience and difficult for us to understand. Why should God be opposed to a woman's wearing male garments (22:5) or to the boiling of a kid in milk drawn from its mother (14:21)? Other laws condone cruelty and utter annihilation of Israel's enemies. Without explaining or defending these commands, I would like to call attention to others which have remarkable relevance for today.

Deuteronomy shows compassion toward the poor. Fellow Israelites who fall into debt are to have their bills cancelled in the year of release, which comes every seven years. But the nearness of this year should not cause anyone to refuse to lend to those in need! (15:1-2, 7-11). The poor are to be allowed to glean in the fields and vineyards after a harvest (24:19-22). A person may take anything from a vineyard or field that he can eat—it only becomes stealing when he tries to carry some home (23:24f). Thus the needs of the poor are met without too much damage to the rights of the wealthy.

Deuteronomy gives rules for the release of fellow Hebrews who have been sold into slavery because of debt. After serving six years, they are to be released with an ample "nest egg" to begin a new life. If the slave chooses to remain with the master, however, provision is made for this (15:12-18). The owner is admonished to remember that he was once a slave in Egypt, or at least his ancestors were. Thus all social classes are transient and relative; we should not take our status in society as seriously as we often do. The Book of Deuteronomy does not abolish classes but seeks to restrain the rich and powerful, while protecting the poor and weak.

A number of seemingly minor rules are to be explained by this concern for the poor. A millstone is not to be taken as a pledge for debt because it is the debtor's only means of earning a living and paying his debt (24:6). A merchant is not to keep one set of weights and measures to use when buying and another for selling (25:13-16). One who goes to take a pledge from a poor man must not show disrespect by entering the man's house uninvited (24:10-11). A hired servant must be paid at the end of each day because he has no surplus from which to pay his expenses (24:14-15). Much is written about the "sojourner" in Deuteronomy. This word refers to the non-Israelites who remained after Canaan was conquered or to their descendants. These persons are to be protected because the Hebrews themselves were once sojourners in Egypt (24:17-18).

Other provisions in Deuteronomy demonstrate sensitivity to the needs and rights of persons. A house must be built with a parapet around the flat roof to prevent falls and injuries (22:8). A newly-married man should remain with his wife for a year before being drafted for war (24:5). A runaway slave is not to be returned but is to be protected and respected (23:15-16). The child of a favorite wife is not to be given a larger legacy than would normally be the case; the rights of the unfavored wife and her child must be respected (21:15-17). If a beautiful woman is taken captive in war, she must be treated according to carefully prescribed rules which protect the woman without abolishing the time-honored custom (21:10-14).

Even criminals are given protection in Deuteronomy. While wrongdoing must be punished, the penalty must be appropriate and limited to what is consistent with reason. If a person kills another by accident, he may flee to a designated city of refuge and escape the revenge of the victim's kinsmen (19:4-10). No one is to be convicted on the evidence of a single witness, and a false witness is to be severely punished (19:15-21). One who is beaten for a crime is to receive no more than forty strokes, lest "your brother be degraded in your sight" (25:3).

In sum, Deuteronomy advocates treating human beings with respect. It even extends the same compassion to birds and oxen (22:6-7; 25:4). Yet, 2,600 years later, we do not show the same concern. I once visited a friend in a county jail and then complained to the sheriff about the inhuman living conditions in it. "We're not running a hotel," he replied. He was running a place of detention for persons who had been *accused,* not yet convicted, of crime. And even those convicted of crime are protected by the constitution against cruel and unusual punishment. Law and human decency require us to treat criminals better than we do. Some demonic power seems to impel us to treat others as servants, as customers, as members of an inferior sex or race, as children, as rivals, as enemies—as anything except full human beings who deserve as much respect as we claim for ourselves. Rooted in an experience of God's gracious acts on behalf of his people, Deuteronomy calls for fair treatment of all persons, whether Hebrews or aliens.

Deuteronomy 21:1-9 has always held special interest for me. An old ordinance from a different culture, it seems to have little relevance for us. But when it is understood and explained in its ancient setting, we may draw a contemporary lesson from it. Ancient people were concerned about guilt, which in Hebrew is literally "blood." Blood is the life of an animal or person, and it seems to continue living when it leaves a body. When blood is shed maliciously, it calls for vengeance. That is how God knew that Cain had slain Abel (Gen. 4:10). Here in Deuteronomy there is concern about the guilt which results from a slain man found in the open country. Our reaction to such an event would be to search for clues and witnesses. If none could be found, we would simply write it off as an unsolved crime. But for the ancient Hebrews it was not that simple. Someone would have to bear the guilt for this crime, if not the actual perpetrator then someone else. Hence, the law provided for determining the nearest city by measurement. The elders of that city then killed a heifer and went through a ceremony of purification.

To me this says that there are no innocent bystanders. We are involved in crime and suffering, whether we recognize the fact or not. In a rural county where I once lived, the residents were horrified when a disturbed woman abandoned her infant son in a snowdrift. Not a month later, however, the same residents turned down a bond issue for mental health in that county. How easily we wash our hands of the problems and misdeeds of others! Yet the fact is that our actions and lack of action are responsible for more evil than we can ever realize or admit. Richard Wright wrote a novel about an enraged black man who killed a white banker's daughter. In the trial it was brought out that the banker, by exploiting the blacks living in his rental properties, had helped to make the killer what he became. Often the respectable citizen, if not directly to blame, is less "innocent" than he appears to be. Deuteronomy 21:1-9 is a call for corporate responsibility. When a crime takes place, we all need to ask, "What did I do, or fail to do? What can I do to prevent that happening again?"

The Importance of Deuteronomy for the Church Today

The prominence of tradition in Deuteronomy should not suggest to us that it is opposed to all change. The book is itself an updating of old traditions. Scarcely had it been discovered when editors began supplementing the book and adapting its principles to new situations. Some sought to interpret the history of Israel and Judah in the light of Deuteronomy. Others challenged the simplistic doctrine of retribution so pervasive in the book. Thus the ancient Hebrew traditions were adapted and revised through the centuries. The way in which this was done throughout the Old and New Testaments is an instructive study. There was concern, on the one hand, to preserve what is old and good. There was readiness, on the other hand, to adapt and even change the old tradition in the light of new experiences and insights.

Paul was subjected to physical abuse and condemnation because he appeared to reject the Jewish religion with its demand for obedience to rules. Paul felt that he had not betrayed the tradition but had found, in its rich diversity, elements which had been neglected. He called for a return to the religion of Abraham, in which grateful response to God's promise was more important than the observance of rules.

The tradition extolled in Deuteronomy is a living force, and all living things are characterized by change. Change must be orderly, of course, and uncontrolled growth of an organism means deadly cancer. But growth and change in keeping with the organism's own nature is healthy and necessary. In *Fiddler on the Roof,* Tevye soon discovers that the old rules do not always fit changing conditions. At last he concedes the right of his three daughters to choose their own husbands. As the play ends, the people of Anatevka are moving out to travel the long road to Palestine, to America, and elsewhere. We sense that their vision has broadened, even though they will not surrender much that is good in their traditional faith. There is change, of course, but there remains a vital memory of what God has done and what we must do.

Now I would like to suggest four implications of Deuteronomy for life in the church today.

1. The first implication is that *old truth may well be the best truth.* We have an obsession about being up-to-date which really means a restless desire for change. We pursue fads in theology, in preaching, in Christian education, and in mission. Many of the things our fathers and grandfathers believed and did were not all that bad. At least, they were not bad simply because our fathers did them. And what we do is not good simply because it is new!

The English writer G. K. Chesterton appealed for what he called a "democracy of the dead." He wanted nobody to be denied a vote in important decisions just because he or she happened to be dead! Maybe that would be putting too heavy a hand of restraint on the present generation. But the idea of consulting our ancestors when in doubt is a good one. We may find that they have faced similar difficulties and can tell us which solutions worked and which did not.

A new respect for our religious heritage would mean a more intense and serious study of the Bible. Of course, it tells of events that happened long ago. Of course, its people did not think as we do. Of course, it takes some effort to understand the Bible and to find its meaning, if any, for today. But valuable things rarely come to us without effort. At the Homestake Mine near Deadwood, South Dakota, I saw the heavy machinery and tons of ore required to produce a few ounces of gold. There is pure gold in the pages of the Bible if we have the patience to look for it and if we are not hampered by the common assumption that what is ancient can have no meaning for us.

2. A second meaning of Deuteronomy is that *old traditions become meaningful when we are able to make them a lively experience in the present.* Remembering the past must be something more than the perfunctory repetition of words. Deuteronomy expresses great concern that God's acts be remembered, not as something that happened to Israel's ancestors but as something in which each succeeding generation participates. The ritual of chapter 26 makes it possible for the worshiper to reenact the drama of redemption and to experience it personally.

One way in which we can experience the past as a present reality is through the Lord's Supper. It should not simply be a habit, a ritual that must be carried out according to prescribed forms. It should be a reenactment of the Last Supper, in which we sense the importance and the deep meaning of the event. Jesus should be the unseen Host who is about to offer himself for us. We are the disciples, and some or all of us have participated in his betrayal. The various festivals of the Christian year—Advent, Epiphany, Holy Week, Pentecost—ought to be explained and dramatized so that the life of the church is nurtured by a cycle of participatory celebrations.

Christian education can make better use of drama as a way of understanding and participating in our heritage of history and faith. Many church groups borrow features of the Jewish Passover meal, with its bitter herbs and unleavened bread, in order to understand the agony of slavery in Egypt and the joy of deliverance. Other biblical stories which lend themselves to dramatization are David's encounter with Nathan after his sin against Uriah, Amos' preaching at Bethel and the argument with Amaziah, Nehemiah's inspection of the walls of Jerusalem and his resolve to rebuild, Jesus' calling of his disciples, and the healing of the lame man by Peter and John. We can dramatize these in the church school, not as entertainment, but as a way of making the ancient stories our own story.

It is my belief that we Christians must rediscover who we are. The way to do this is to restore our links with the events and religious experiences of our past so that they become, in a real sense, our own. Biology shows that we carry in our genes a physical heritage that comes to us through a thousand generations. Our religious heritage is passed on only by conscious effort. It is always in danger of being lost through neglect.

3. A third implication of Deuteronomy is *our need to rediscover what it means to be the people of God.* In the Hebrew-Christian tradition, religion is first of all a corporate experience. The individual knows and serves God as a member of the believing community. Temple, synagogue, and church are essential elements, though not the totality, of religious expression.

In the 1940s and 1950s, there was a strong interest in the church among American Protestants. The growth of the ecumenical movement and the resurgence of biblical theology had much to do with this. In the 1960s and 1970s, this churchly interest has waned. Many councils of churches have declined in strength or have been disbanded. The mainline churches have gone down in membership and financial strength. The struggles for civil rights and against war have alienated both those who felt that the church was too involved and those who felt that it was too little involved. There is a new interest in religion today, but often it takes the form of individual piety, sect groups on the fringes of the church, or syncretistic cults strongly flavored with eastern mysticism. There are few signs at this writing that the church is recovering its honored place as the heir of our biblical heritage and the locus of God's self-disclosure.

I think we need to rediscover the church as the people of God. We can do this by a study of Deuteronomy and other parts of the Bible which stress this theme. We can do it by a serious study of the long history of the church, with all of its triumphs and failures. We can do it by a new stress on the community in worship and Christian education. We can do it by becoming aware of what we have in common with other Christians, Catholic and Protestant. We do not need to glamorize the people of God or gloss over their failures. Deuteronomy does not do that. Instead, we can focus on the people of God as the recipients of God's grace, called to responsible service and not to any form of arrogant self-righteousness or exclusivism.

4. A final implication of Deuteronomy, as I understand it, is *the grounding of ethics in the faith about God's saving acts.* The book is full of rules for living, but all of them are related to what God has done or will do. The imperative grows out of the indicative. The Israelites are called on to treat their fellows, and even aliens, as human beings because they themselves were once slaves and now have been set free.

One reason that we have difficulty deciding right and wrong today is that our ethical reasoning is no longer grounded in an experience of salvation. Even in the church we are told to do certain things only because they will somehow benefit us and other persons. Sometimes we are told to support causes already proclaimed by society at large (feminism, peace, civil rights) because the church must not be the last group to discover their merits. In short, our ethical teaching derives from worldly prudence and not from a distinctive faith.

We Christians need to recover a lively sense of what God has done for us and for all mankind in Jesus Christ. "God shows his love for us in that while we were yet sinners Christ died for us" (Rom. 5:8). If we really understand and believe that, we need not ask why it is imperative to show love toward our neighbors. We will both know what we need to do and have a reason for doing it.

Chapter 10

How to Read and Enjoy the Bible

In my mind's eye, I can see someone reading this book and deciding that Bible study can be exciting. He or she goes to the church library and opens a book about the Bible. The reader quickly finds a number of strange words like "apocalyptic" and "existential." He or she may even find a lot of Hebrew and Greek words in the book. The reader quickly puts the book down in disappointment and frustration, wanting to grow in understanding of the Bible but unable to handle difficult books about the Bible. If this happens to you, don't give up!

Bible study can be compared to music. There are persons who give their lives to the study of music, and we make grateful use of their skills. Though we are not as skillful or knowledgeable as these persons, we can still enjoy music in our own way. We can listen to music we like and even learn to play instruments. We recognize that we are only amateurs, but this does not keep us from enjoying and improving our musical skills. In the same way, I believe, we can improve our understanding and use of the Bible without attempting to do what a Bible scholar does and without becoming frustrated because we cannot do so.

Choosing Your Area of Competence

It is important to understand the different *areas of competence* in Bible study and to select the one in which you feel most comfortable. I believe it is helpful to delineate four of these, even though there is much overlapping among them.

Area A. Persons who select this area may spend several hours a week reading a good translation of the Bible. They may have one or two good reference works in addition to the Bible. They know where to find passages in the Old and New Testaments. Some of these persons find value in memorizing parts of the Scriptures. I am often amazed by how much such persons know about what is in the Bible.

Area B. Persons who select this area know how to find good reference works about the Bible and how to use them. Sometimes these persons teach the Bible in the church school, but they also study it in order to grow as Christians. This group is different from the first group because its members are well acquainted with books about the Bible as well as the Bible itself.

Area C. This group of persons is different from the first two in having had college or seminary training in Bible study. Such persons are usually full-time religious workers or ministers who spend part of their time interpreting the Bible. Some of them may have studied Hebrew and/or Greek.

Area D. These are persons who spend all their working time studying and interpreting the Bible. Such persons must know several languages and be proficient in history, linguistics, archeology, and other sciences. Most such Bible scholars specialize in the Old or the New Testament.

I know and respect persons in all of these four areas of competence. It is important to decide which of these we want to pursue, and then we can concentrate on improving our skills *within the area of competence we have chosen.* We need not feel frustrated because we cannot do something that a person in some other area can do. I can learn more about the history of Baroque music and even play simple tunes on my recorder, even though I know that I will never perform in concert.

Improving Your Competence as a Bible Student

I have called these four fields of study *areas* rather than levels of competence because I do not believe they are stages in growth. Ordinarily, one chooses an area and stays in it for a number of years, even a lifetime. One area is not "better" than another, though a person in one of these areas may be "better" and more skillful than he or she was last year. I want now to suggest some things you can do to grow in Areas A or B. Those who choose Areas C or D will look elsewhere for guidance.

A person who chooses Area A should select one translation of the Bible and stay with it. My first choice would be the *Revised Standard Version,* and my second choice would be the *New English Bible.* Both of these are close to the best manuscripts of Hebrew, Aramaic, and Greek. Both are understandable to the twentieth-century reader. In the section following, I will explain how to compare and use different translations.

A person who chooses Area A should also have one or two good reference books to help in understanding difficult passages.

My first choice would be *Peake's Commentary on the Bible.*[1] I would also suggest that Bible readers in this area of competence keep a notebook of what they have learned. After studying a psalm, a parable, or a chapter from the Old or New Testament, they should make some notes under these headings:

A. Helps for Understanding This Scripture

B. What This Scripture Says to Me About My Life Today

A person who chooses Area B will need to know something about other books besides the Bible. The books listed here should be found in a good church library, and the student may also wish to purchase some of them. A Bible atlas helps one to understand the history and geography of the Bible. My first choice would be the colorful *Golden Bible Atlas.*[2] *The Westminster Historical Atlas to the Bible* is also valuable, though not as interesting.[3] Bible Dictionaries provide short articles on many important subjects. *The New Westminster Dictionary of the Bible* is a good basic Bible dictionary.[4] *The Interpreter's Dictionary of the Bible,* in four volumes, provides more comprehensive treatment but may tell you more than you want to know.[5] A real bargain is *A Theological Word Book of the Bible,*[6] now available in paper. This book can be used by the lay person in doing word studies.

The person who chooses Area B needs also to know and to use one or more books which provide an overview of the Bible as a whole. A good one with which to begin is *The Unfolding Drama of the Bible* by Bernard W. Anderson.[7] Another is *The Book of the Acts of God* by G. E. Wright and R. H. Fuller.[8] More detailed information is given in *Introduction to the Bible* by John H. Hayes[9] and *The Heritage of Biblical Faith* by J. P. Hyatt.[10] The recently published *Abingdon Bible Handbook,* though expensive, provides a wealth of material in readable form.[11]

There are a number of commentaries available, only a few of which may be used profitably by persons in Area B. *The Daily Study Bible* by William Barclay[12] is lively and interesting, though the author is more conservative than I am about the authorship and date of books of the Bible. *Peake's Commentary on the Bible* is the best one-volume commentary I have found.[1] *The Layman's Bible Commentary* is an excellent, readable collection.[13] *The Interpreter's Bible* provides a mass of information in twelve volumes.[14] You will find some help in the general articles in Volumes 1, 7, and 12, though some may be "over your head." You may find some help in the introductions to individual books and the comments on various chapters of the Bible, especially the readable "exposition" section at the bottom of each page.

There is a great mass of material on the Bible available, much of it trivial, inaccurate, and misleading. It is important to ask not only how much the author knows but what his or her point of view is. Does the writer think of the Bible as so different from other books that the methods used by historians do not apply to it? Or does the writer think of the Bible as a book that may be investigated and understood in much the same way as other ancient writings are studied? The books that I recommend here generally represent the second point of view.

The lay reader can find books that conform to the open and investigative point of view by noting the name of the publisher. Books published by Westminster, Abingdon, John Knox, Harper, Doubleday, Macmillan, Nelson, and Oxford University Press are generally reliable. This is simply a rule-of-thumb, and there will be many exceptions to it. These publishers will sometimes put out a poor book, and other publishers will market good ones.

Why study the Bible? Some time ago there appeared in the press the story of a convict who had memorized whole books of the Bible. He was released after serving his term but was shortly returned for breaking the law. Study of the Bible was for him apparently only a way to pass the time. Others might study the book in order to win arguments, to impress others, or to get a professor's post.

There are many who read the Bible in order to hear the voice of God, in order to be aware of God's self-disclosure and respond to it in an appropriate manner. There are those who believe the Bible holds answers to the most significant issues of life: Why are we here? What are we to do? Where do we go from here? What really matters? For these persons there are vital reasons for studying the Bible, and their concern is abundantly rewarded.

Once I moved to a new city. It was important for me to learn the major highways and streets of the area immediately. It was not necessary for me to visit or know all the thousands of streets and neighborhoods, but I did have to learn how to get to work, how to get home, and where the best stores were located. Eventually, I hope to explore some interesting areas in detail.

The student must approach the Bible in much the same way. In order to understand any part of it he or she must have some general understanding of the book as a whole. He or she must have an acquaintance with several important parts of it. He or she must know where to turn for information in the Bible and about the Bible. This does not mean that the student must know all parts of the Bible equally well. Even scholars who devote full time to a study of the Bible do not attempt to become experts on all of it. If we can become well acquainted with one or two books at first, we can add other parts of the Bible to our growing awareness as the years pass.

The Bible was not written consecutively from Genesis to Revelation, and there is no reason it must be read this way. A person may choose to read an Old Testament book and then a New Testament book. One may choose to study a book from each testament at the same time. There are other possible patterns. For maximum learning, it is important to study those portions which are of greatest interest first.

Which books of the Bible are most important? Which should be studied most carefully? Everyone who reads the Bible will have favorite parts, those which speak most effectively to her or his needs.

Personally, I have ten favorites among the thirty-nine Old Testament books: five prophetic books and five other books. These are: Isaiah, Jeremiah, Ezekiel, Amos, Hosea, Genesis, Exodus, Deuteronomy, Job, and Psalms. Among the twenty-seven New Testament books, I am most interested in the Gospels, Acts, and the letters of Paul (Romans, 1 and 2 Corinthians, Galatians, Philippians, Colossians, 1 and 2 Thessalonians, Philemon).

The student needs to know these basic facts about each book in which he or she does intensive investigation: What is known about how this came to be written and who wrote it? What do we know about the time *in which* it was written? If it contains history of the past, what is known about the time *about which* it was written? What are the main ideas about God and man expressed in this book? Other information may also be important, depending on which book of the Bible is being studied.

Most books of the Bible are readily subdivided into paragraphs or sections. A reader may examine one of these at a time, keeping notes on what he or she discovers about each. Let us suppose, for example, that Luke 4:16-30 is being studied.

The student notes first that this is in the Gospel of Luke, written some fifty years after the crucifixion of Jesus by a writer who also edited the Book of Acts. While the writer apparently did not know Jesus personally, he may have known persons who did. He himself states that many others had already written about Jesus, and he used some of these written sources to compose his Gospel. His purpose was to present Christianity in a favorable light to some persons who may have heard false rumors about it. He also sought to show the broad sympathy for all persons which characterized Jesus.

With these background notes in mind, we may turn to the

130

passage being studied. The student may wish to write down a number of phrases which point to the content of this section:

—Jesus was customarily in the synagogue on the sabbath
—A hometown boy goes to his old church
—Jesus knew the Old Testament, his Bible
—Here is a passage he loved
—The passage he quoted speaks of the Spirit at work
—Jesus felt set apart for a task
—He felt called to help persons, to give them hope
—Reactions to Jesus: surprise, then anger
—Why his own neighbors rejected Jesus

These and other phrases may help the reader to discover the essential elements of this section of Luke. After this has been done, the reader should list a number of possible meanings which the scripture might have for her or him. These may include the following:

—My search for a task worth doing
—The importance of serving persons
—How Bible texts guide my life
—Why I admire and appreciate Jesus
—I must expect to be misunderstoond and rejected by some

Thus the study of this particular section has included three essential elements:

1. What we need to know about the section (background)
2. What the scripture says (content)
3. What the scripture means for me (significance)

It is important for a reader to consult commentaries and also to spend adequate time considering and perhaps recording personal impressions of each section of the Bible studied. In this way he or she is able to make the studies a living and vital experience in his or her own life rather than something simply read or read about.

It is not necessary to know Hebrew and Greek or to have access to a seminary library in order to do important research on Bible problems. A student may not discover anything not already known to scholars, but he may become aware of many biblical themes of first importance to himself. In addition, the student will have the satisfaction of having gone beyond the obvious in a search for greater understanding of the Bible.

In the passage just studied, for example, Jesus used a part of the Old Testament. With what parts of the Old Testament was Jesus familiar, and how did he use them? Did he ever reject any of the Old Testament as unacceptable and unworthy of his respect? Did he regard it as infallible? If he selected certain parts of it for special attention, which did he choose? Why did he choose these?

Many editions of the Gospels indicate what verses are quoted from the Old Testament and where the original text may be found. By going through each of the Gospels, a reader may make notes on these quotations and compare them. Answers to our questions about how Jesus used the Old Testament should emerge from this study. It should also give us some guidance in our own use (or misuse) of scripture.

Here are some other problems into which the laymen may delve profitably:

—What Genesis 1—3 says about man's relationship to his environment
—A list of characteristics of Abraham
—Sex ethics and ideals implied in the Book of Judges
—What God did for Israel, according to Deuteronomy
—The rights of minorities in Deuteronomy
—The attitudes of Amos toward poor and rich
—Images of hope in Isaiah 40—66
—What God is like, according to the Psalms
—The teachings of Jesus about marriage
—How Jesus understood his mission, according to the Gospel of Luke
—What Paul wrote about women
—What the Book of James understands by "faith"

These are a few examples of the kinds of problems which will occur to the alert Bible reader. She or he will want to begin by stating and defining the problem. If he tries to do too much, he will lose interest before the study is finished. Also, the study should not be trivial or obscure. For maximum learning and the continued desire to pursue such studies, the student should select subjects which might have a bearing on his or her own beliefs and behavior.

Understanding of the Bible is often enhanced by pursuing a single word or theme through several books or the whole Bible. Many Christians today have an interest in the Spirit and its effects upon persons. How does the Spirit work? What does it cause persons to do? What dangers are involved in it? One may find the answers to these questions by looking up the word in a concordance or Bible dictionary. Of particular interest is the use of the word in Acts and the letters of Paul. Among other discoveries one may make is the fact that Paul had reservations about "speaking in tongues" and other gifts of the Spirit when they were not accompanied by self-control and love. He seemed to favor what we might call "the gentle gifts of the Spirit" (Gal. 5:22-23).

One problem which the student encounters is that several Hebrew or Greek words may be translated by the same English word. Also, a single Hebrew or Greek word may be translated with different English words or phrases, depending on the context. Thus *ruach* may mean either "breath," "wind," or "spirit." This means that simply looking up English words in a concordance may be confusing and misleading. The simplest way to escape this confusion is to follow the guidance of a Bible dictionary or word book. One of the best is *A Theological Word Book of the Bible*.[6] This book tells what words are used to express an idea and gives a selection of references in the Old and New Testaments which we may examine for further enlightenment.

The individual should devise a program of study which best meets personal needs. The result should be an acquaintance with many parts of the Bible, an awareness of the book as a whole, a confidence that one has begun to understand the message of scripture, and a greater awareness of God's self-disclosure both in ancient times and today. Some of the pressing problems of today are these: What is the importance of the world of nature and how should man relate to it? What is the future of man? How can we decide matters of right and wrong? Who is God and what does he expect of us? All of us form some answers to these questions, explicit or hidden, because we must all act on the basis of such answers. Those who ponder the Bible thoughtfully will have a special source of guidance in making decisions based on reason and faith.

Translations and Paraphrases

Our generation has seen the publication of many English translations, and some of them have enjoyed phenomenal sale. Some of these depart from the Hebrew and Greek text to an alarming degree. Many lay persons enjoy reading such translations and paraphrases and seem to choose a favorite on the basis of whether or not it "sounds good." If this is the only criterion of value, then anyone can write a Bible and we can dispense with a lot of useless scholarship! If it is important to discover the most reliable texts in the original languages and if it is important to translate them accurately and understandably, then there is work to do, and lay persons should recognize and appreciate good work.

About 1950, a young person asked me, "Is it all right to neck if you know what you're doing?" The question seemed odd, but it concealed a special wisdom. It is all right to do some things if we have our thoughts and emotions under full control. And it is

133

all right to paraphrase the Bible if we know what we are doing. Paraphrasing is often a helpful way to illuminate a text, but we should always recognize that this is a departure from the original and must be used with caution.

Translating the Bible must go on because the meanings of words change. An old translation may have been good in its day, but it is now misleading. The *King James Version* of 1 Corinthians 15: 33 reads: "Evil communications corrupt good manners." In the seventeenth century this referred to associating and conversing with other persons. Recently I heard a preacher use this text to criticize sex and violence on television! His point may have been well taken, but it had little to do with 1 Corinthians 15:33.

Even the best translation is always a compromise. The more accurate it is, the more difficult it is to read. A literal, word-for-word rendering has little or no meaning. The more lively and appealing a translation becomes, as a rule, the more it departs from what is known to scholars about the original text. A free translation or paraphrase becomes a kind of commentary in which the translator provides a running interpretation of the text. The commentary may be accurate, but other commentators may have a different view. Wouldn't it usually be better to leave the Bible text as it is and supply the comments in a separate book or section? Then the reader could accept or reject the latter.

Here is a comparison of different translations of Philippians 3: 14, in which Paul explains his own view of the future. The Greek may be literally rendered: "toward the goal I seek to the prize of the upper call of God in Christ Jesus." Clearly, the translator will need to do some shifting of words and interpreting in order to make sense out of this in English. The question is: How much interpretation should be given?

The *King James Version* is good in this instance: "I press toward the mark for the prize of the high calling of God in Christ Jesus." The *Revised Standard Version* only changes "mark" to "goal" and "high calling" to "upward call."

This is a good rendering of the Greek, but it leaves some unanswered questions. What is the goal or prize? What does the phrase "in Christ Jesus" mean? And the most puzzling word is the Greek *ano* which literally means "upper." What is God's "upper call"?

Phillips understood *ano* to mean honor. He translated freely: "I go straight for the goal—my reward the honour of my high calling by God in Christ Jesus."[15] This is an interesting interpretation but by no means the only possible one.

Some translations suggest a call by God to a better life in this world. Clarence Jordan's paraphrase is: "I push on with all I've got toward the prize of God's invitation to the high road in Christ Jesus."[16]

By contrast, *The Living Bible* gives the text an otherworldly orientation: "I strain to reach the end of the race and receive the prize for which God is calling us up to heaven because of what Christ Jesus did for us."[17] It should be noted that the Greek word for "heaven," *ouranos,* is not in the original text of Philippians 3:14. Paul may have been writing about life after death, but that is a matter of inference, not obvious fact. Paul used the word "heaven" sparingly for some reason. In Romans 8 he wrote about the Christian's hope for eternal fellowship with God without once mentioning heaven. If I had questions or doubts about the nature of heaven, I might find the writings of Paul very helpful. But if I had only *The Living Bible* as a guide, I might be put off by an erroneous reading of Philippians 3:14. This departure from the original is typical of *The Living Bible,* which is occasionally interesting but frequently too uninhibited in its treatment of the text.

Then what did Paul mean by God's "upward call"? Probably we will never know for sure. Two translations suggest something beyond this life but avoid the gratuitous introduction of the concept of heaven. Both the *New English Bible*[18] and *Today's English Version*[19] speak of "God's call to the life above."

Using the Bible Responsibly

A wise old professor opened his beginning lecture in medicine by telling the students, "First: don't do the patient harm." A responsible doctor learns not to prescribe whatever pill comes to mind. And responsible students of the Bible learn early that they cannot assume anything about it that they choose to assume or say anything regarding the Bible that suits their whims.

1. To use the Bible responsibly, we must *view each part of it in relation to other parts and to the Bible as a whole.*

On our living-room table many years ago stood a small container bearing the words "Honey in the Rock." In it were hundreds of small cards, each bearing a Bible verse. Every day we took one out and read it. Often the verse seemed to have some bearing on what was happening that day, but we did not really understand the verse or the book from which it came.

Romans 13:1 states: "Let every person be subject to the governing authorities." Does it mean that a Christian should never oppose those in office? If that is what it means, the verse goes contrary to the words and deeds of Moses, Nathan, Elijah, Amos, Isaiah, Jeremiah, Jesus, John the Baptist, Peter, and John the disciple. Scholars tell us that Paul wrote this advice partly because Roman officials protected him against his enemies. Would he have written the same thing a little later, after seeing what the Romans under Nero did to Christians? In any case, Christians today are not to guide their political behavior on a single verse taken in isolation from the rest of Scripture.

In the Gospel of John, Jesus is reported to have said, "The poor you always have with you" (12:8). Does this mean that Jesus felt there was nothing we could do to alleviate poverty? If so, we must disregard several parables and teachings of Jesus found elsewhere in the Gospels. We must assume that he was heartless, callous, and pessimistic. Actually, scholars have shown that many of the teachings of Jesus are no longer accompanied by the original situation or question to which they were addressed. This means that we do not know exactly what Jesus may have meant when and if he spoke these words. Again, it is a mistake to draw any conclusion from a single saying of Jesus separated from his life and other reported teachings.

A single verse or chapter of the Bible may mislead us unless we compare it with other parts of Scripture. The entire New Testament, in fact, is incomplete without the Old Testament. The Messiah, the people of God, the Law, Spirit, and love are only a few ideas found in the New Testament which have earlier roots in Hebrew writings.

Since about 1920, much writing about the Bible has emphasized its oneness. It is not simply a chance collection of essentially unrelated fragments. It is one people's continuing and changing experience of God through more than a thousand years. To see this total sweep in all of its dimensions is an enlightening and awe-inspiring experience. We sense the presence of a God who seeks to disclose himself, wrestling with persons and their limitations, speaking clearly to them, then withdrawing so that they may be free to respond to what they have heard.

The Bible is an intensely human book. This means more than the fact that it contains errors. It means that the book introduces us to a living encounter between man and man and between man and God. The Bible is not a series of words and statements, frozen for all eternity just as they have come down to us. When we read the words of the Bible with an open mind and heart, we sense a presence within and beyond the words, a presence which encounters and challenges us in our time. J. B. Phillips described his experience of translating the New Testament as somewhat like wiring a house with the current turned on!

The Bible is a single book which relates one people's continuing experience of God, an experience into which we also may enter when we read the Bible responsibly. In spite of this oneness, the Bible shows some important internal differences which we must note in order to understand it. We find remarkable divergences, for example, between Genesis 1 and Genesis 2, between Amos and Second Isaiah, between the first three Gospels and the fourth, between the letters of Paul and the Book of James. When we are aware of these divergences, they fascinate and enlighten us. The Bible becomes, not a static statement of what we must believe but a dynamic exploration of changing reality through a series of developing experiences. God speaks to us in our own situation as we see the varying ways in which he spoke to ancient men and women.

We cannot hope, of course, to take the whole Bible into account every time we read a single verse. We can, however, be familiar with many parts of it and have a basic understanding of the total book. Only then do the individual parts assume their proper significance for us. We should also make a special effort to examine, from time to time, parts of the Bible which are less familiar to us.

2. To use the Bible responsibly, we must *view each part in the light of what we know about how it came to be written and what it originally meant.* This means we must go outside the Bible itself for assistance from competent scholars who have studied ancient history and the books of the Bible in their original Hebrew, Aramaic, and Greek.

Responsible use of the Bible requires us to use the best information about it which is available to us today. In the same way, a doctor who prescribes a pill will take into account what competent and careful researchers have discovered about its effects. In fact, biblical scholars proceed in much the same way as do scientists who test drugs. All the known facts relating to a problem about the Bible are carefully weighed and a tentative conclusion drawn. The conclusion is published, and other scholars react to it. If an idea withstands the test of many years of study and it is the one which best fits the facts available, scholars assume it to be reasonably correct.

When a person studies any portion of scripture, he or she needs to look for a few important facts: What do we know about the person who wrote this? When was it written? What were some of the purposes of the author? What did the words and phrases mean when first used? If there is uncertainty among scholars about these, this should be pointed out.

If a person were to study the first chapter of Genesis, for example, she or he might consult the *Interpreter's One Volume Commentary on the Bible.*[20] On pages 1-5 he would discover that Genesis is a compilation of three different traditions which were written over a period of four centuries or more. Chapter 1 comes from the P strand, written after 539 B.C. and closely related to Babylonian creation stories. Among other things, the investigator would learn that the word "day" probably meant the same thing we usually mean by it. The word "firmament" describes the translucent dome which covers the earth and to which the lights of heaven are attached, according to ancient belief. While we ourselves may not believe the earth is flat or that the world was created in six days, we must recognize that the person who wrote this account probably did so. A few basic facts about this chapter are not all that is needed in order to understand it, but they are a necessary beginning toward such an understanding.

3. To use the Bible responsibly, *we must allow it to speak to us instead of trying to make it say what we want it to say.*

It is understandable that those who know little about the Bible should have mistaken views of its message. But they are not the only ones who mute its message. Teachers, ministers, and scholars, some of whom have studied the book for many years, use it irresponsibly by twisting its truth. In a class session or a sermon, we often seek those scriptures which support the view we "want to get across." We unconsciously neglect those parts of the Bible which present a different view.

What does the Bible say about man's use of his environment? What does it say about the role of women? What does it say about abortion? About man's future? These are only a few of the questions being asked by thoughtful persons when they open the Bible today. It will speak to these issues if we allow it to do so, if we listen attentively. But it will not always say what we expect or want to hear. The alert reader, even one who has studied the Bible carefully for years, will ask these questions afresh as he or she studies the book, prepared to be surprised by the findings.

The Swiss theologian Karl Barth noted that the Bible is "an eternally living thing . . . continually presenting itself to different ages and men from new angles, in new dimensions and with a new aspect."[21] It breaks out of all the narrow rooms into which we try to force it and in which we try to preserve it. It is a living power confronting man. It is not a dead text which lies harmlessly between book covers, nor is it a collection of words which we can manipulate and arrange to suit our purposes. The Bible seeks us and speaks to us about God in our time. The responsible student of the Bible tries to hear what it has to say.

4. To use the Bible responsibly, *we must be aware of our own bias regarding it*. No one approaches the Bible with complete objectivity. Everyone has certain assumptions and preconceived ideas about the book. Everyone has an axe to grind when he takes up the Bible. The late Reinhold Niebuhr recognized this. He said that he never left the pulpit without asking God's forgiveness for the unintended and unconscious ways in which he had distorted the scripture. No one can read or interpret it, he felt, without imposing his own views upon it.

This is not altogether bad. Even if it were possible to be uninvolved and dispassionate when reading the Bible, this would not help us to understand it. The Bible itself is a book of faith, and no one can rightly grasp its meaning unless he or she also is a person of faith. Because it was written by and for the committed, we must stand within the circle of the committed in order to interpret scripture. One who speaks with full authority about marriage must experience it from within. One who understands the message of the Bible must share something of the sense of wonder and the life commitment which characterized those who wrote and preserved it for us.

Before reading the Bible again, write out what you believe about God, about the Bible, about Jesus, about the church, about right and wrong, about the way in which God communicates with persons. These are your biases, your beliefs. They will tend to color your understanding of the Bible as well as other experiences. If you can express these beliefs and admit them, they will have less power to distort your vision. Instead of contributing to your misinterpretation of the Bible, they will help you to approach it responsibly. After reading the Bible and listening to it speaking to you, take another look at these beliefs and see whether you wish to change them.

This chapter points to a number of ways in which persons tend to misuse the Bible—by taking parts out of context, by neglecting the known facts about it, by making it say what we want it to say. This word of caution is necessary, but it should not discourage us from studying the Bible at all. There are some things we should not do when driving a car, but this does not mean we should never drive.

The Bible Reveals God

Is God like a kind father or like a stern judge? Is he a process or a person? Is he like man and, if so, in what way? Does God hate sinners or love them? What does God expect those who serve him to do? How may we appropriately worship God?

By lifting out single verses and chapters, one could find a variety of answers to each of these questions. But if one views the Bible as a whole, and sees Jesus Christ as its center, there is a fairly clear answer about what God is like. God is the Creator of all that is. He has made man in such a way that he is able to communicate with man. He is infinitely concerned for the welfare of all his creatures. He gives himself freely for them. He promises them life in him if they will receive it, the only complete life they can hope to have. God makes promises and keeps them. He has many good things in store for those who seek him.

If these few sentences are what the Bible is all about, why take sixty-six books to say it? Because the truth of the Bible cannot be reduced to this or any other formula. In fact, even the sixty-six books do not express the message of the Bible. God does not reveal himself in words but in human experience. He reveals himself in victory and defeat, in wisdom and foolishness, in good times and bad. Why does it take so long for God to say what he has to say? Because men will not listen until events have prepared them to do so. For centuries the prophets tried to tell Israel and Judah of their wrongs, but only when the two nations were destroyed were they taken seriously. The message of Jesus, the culmination of the Bible, had to be incarnated in the life and death of a person. Nothing less would communicate the word of God.

Some persons may read the Bible and fail to notice anything unusual about it. For my part, I have continually been amazed by this book. I sense the presence of God at work within and behind these pages. My study leads me to believe that God did not override or cancel out the ignorance and limitations of the persons who wrote scripture. If he had done this, they would presumably agree with each other. They would understand all science and all history, as God does. Their religious ideas would show a monotonous sameness instead of the rich variety they now display. But even though God did not choose to work through these writers by simply telling them what to write, he discloses himself through them nevertheless.

How does God disclose himself to men? In Jeremiah's case, he spoke through a reluctant prophet. Jeremiah did not want to hear and speak the word of God. He asked to be excused. He was not a very pious man. He almost blew the opportunity God gave to him.

God spoke to Jeremiah in several ways. In one case, the prophet happened to notice a potter working with some clay. As often happens, the clay did not take the form intended by the potter, and he started over again. Jeremiah suddenly realized that God

140

could do the same thing with his erring people! An ordinary event carried an important message which Jeremiah and others needed to learn.

God speaks to us in daily events—a sickness, a visit from a friend, a change of jobs, a trip to the mountains. Through these events God may tell us to take it easy, to trust in him, to love others, and to change our course. What God says to us in these everyday events will be partly dependent on our previous experiences with God, on our sharing the faith of the believing community, on our reading of the Bible. We can hear God's voice because he has continually spoken to others in the past and because we enter into the heritage they have left to us. This is why we need to know the Bible, so that God can disclose himself to us through it and in the many other ways he used in addition to the Bible.

The Circle of Understanding

We will not fully appreciate or understand the Bible until we recognize God at work in it. This means that we approach the book somewhat in the spirit of Moses taking off his shoes when he heard the voice of God. The Bible is a book to be studied carefully, in the knowledge that we are here dealing with sacred matters. We here meet the one who holds the key to our own well-being and destiny because he made us and because he alone can remake us. We approach the Bible with knees bent, mind alert, and heart uplifted.

After describing detailed rules for understanding the Bible, Alexander Campbell stressed that it is not enough to know the Bible and the rules for its interpretation. We must sense the presence of God in it if we would fully grasp its significance:

"We must come within the understanding distance.

"There is a distance which is properly called the speaking distance, or the hearing distance, beyond which the voice reaches not, and the ear hears not. To hear another, we must come within that circle which the voice audibly fills.

"Now we may with propriety say, that as it respects God, there is an understanding distance. All beyond that distance cannot understand God; all within it can easily understand him in all matters of piety and morality. God himself is the centre of that circle, and humility is its circumference. . . . He, then, who would interpret the oracles of God to the salvation of his soul, must approach this volume with the humility and docility of a child, and meditate upon it day and night."[22]

141

Notes

Chapter 1

1. For readable discussions of the Letter to Philemon, see William Barclay, *The Letters to Timothy, Titus and Philemon* in the Daily Study Bible Series. Westminister Press, 1960, pp. 309-324. See also the remarks by Holmes Rolston in the *Layman's Bible Commentary* ed. by Balmer H. Kelly. John Knox Press, 1963, Vol. 23, pp. 126-131.
2. The fact that Onesimus fled to Paul suggests that the two men had met earlier, but Paul says in Philemon 10 that Onesimus became a Christian only after coming to Paul in prison.
3. Writing in *The Interpreter's Bible* ed. by G. A. Buttrick; Abingdon, 1955; Vol. 11, pp. 555-573, John Knox argues that Philemon may have been written from Ephesus rather than Rome.
4. See Barclay, *op. cit.,* p. 309.
5. G. K. Chesterton, *Robert Browning.* London: The Macmillan Company 1936, p. 52.
6. For a discussion of the relation between the Letter to Philemon and Bishop Onesimus of Ephesus, see Knox, *op. cit.,* pp. 557-560.
7. Ignatius to the Ephesians, 1:2-3. *The Library of Christian Classics,* ed. by Cyril C. Richardson. The Westminster Press, 1953, Vol. 1, p. 82.
8. For a full discussion, see *The Interpreter's Bible,* Vol. 11, pp. 3-14 and *The Interpreter's Dictionary of the Bible,* ed. by G. A. Buttrick. Abingdon, 1962. Vol. 3, pp. 786-791.
9. "Rejoice" occurs nine times. "Joy" occurs five times.
10. *The New English Bible.* © The Delegates of the Oxford University Press and The Syndics of the Cambridge University Press, 1970. Reprinted by permission.
11. "To Please His Wife" from *Life's Little Ironies.*

Chapter 2

1. A readable explanation of Genesis 1—3 is found in Charles T. Fritch, *The Book of Genesis* (The Layman's Bible Commentary), John Knox Press, 1959, pp. 7-34. A longer and more exhaustive treatment is found in *The Interpreter's Bible,* edited by G. A. Buttrick, Abingdon, 1952, Vol. 1. pp. 458-516. An explanation of the origin of the Book of Genesis is found in the same volume, pp. 439-457. A scholarly and incisive treatment of the early chapters of Genesis is found in Gerhard von Rad, *Genesis: A Commentary,* Westminster Press, 1973.

Chapter 3

1. There is an abundance of material about prophecy and the individual Old Testament prophets. I would avoid books that are too technical or difficult. They could sour you on the whole undertaking and keep you